D060113D

Creative Quilts
FROM YOUR
Crayon Box

Melt-n-Blend Meets Fusible Appliqué

Terrie Linn Kygar

Martingale
Create with Confidence

Dedication

To my mom, Dona, and her mother, Thelma; they taught me so much.

Dona M. Russ: Mom helped teach me how to sew, made special dresses for me and my little sisters, and taught me how to make my first quilt for my first baby. She taught me how to be a mother. Thanks, Mom; I love you.

Thelma J. Smith: Grandma first taught me how to sew and quilt. She sewed the beautiful dresses I wore for almost every special occasion in my life, including my wedding dress. Thanks, Grandma; I love you.

Creative Quilts from Your Crayon Box:
Melt-n-Blend Meets Fusible Appliqué
© 2012 by Terrie Linn Kygar

Martingale®
19021 120th Ave. NE, Ste. 102
Bothell, WA 98011-9511 USA
ShopMartingale.com

No part of this product may be reproduced in any form, unless otherwise stated, in which case reproduction is limited to the use of the purchaser. The written instructions, photographs, designs, projects, and patterns are intended for the personal, noncommercial use of the retail purchaser and are under federal copyright laws; they are not to be reproduced by any electronic, mechanical, or other means, including informational storage or retrieval systems, for commercial use. Permission is granted to photocopy patterns for the personal use of the retail purchaser. Attention teachers: Martingale encourages you to use this book for teaching, subject to the restrictions stated above.

The information in this book is presented in good faith, but no warranty is given nor results guaranteed. Since Martingale has no control over choice of materials or procedures, the company assumes no responsibility for the use of this information.

Printed in China
17 16 15 14 13 12   8 7 6 5 4 3 2

Library of Congress Cataloging-in-Publication Data is available upon request.
ISBN: 978-1-60468-080-5

Mission Statement
Dedicated to providing quality products and service to inspire creativity.

Credits
President & CEO: Tom Wierzbicki
Editor in Chief: Mary V. Green
Design Director: Paula Schlosser
Managing Editor: Karen Costello Soltys
Technical Editor: Nancy Mahoney
Copy Editor: Sheila Chapman Ryan
Production Manager: Regina Girard
Cover & Text Designer: Adrienne Smitke
Illustrator: Laurel Strand
Photographer: Brent Kane

Acknowledgments

Sylvia Dorney, owner of Greenbaum's Quilted Forest in Salem, Oregon, and Rachel Greco, owner of Grandma's Attic in Dallas, Oregon, are women I admire and have had the privilege of working for. They have given me self-confidence and encouragement; I couldn't have done this book without them. Thanks, Sylvia and Rachel.

I would also like to say thanks to:

* Lisa Encabo, for your honesty and generosity in taking the time to help me write better instructions

* Martha, from In House Designs, for helping me name my coloring technique and for making my patterns look beautiful

* Beth Blevins and "The Forest" staff, for going out of your way to promote my classes and the Melt-n-Blend technique

* Arlene Dalton, for helping me write better instructions, and for your time and honesty

* Donna Wheeler, for blessing me with the gift of your beautiful hand-dyed fabric and your enthusiasm

* Karla Alexander and Jody Houghton, for your time and the gift of "peace of mind"

* Linda Perry and Kathy Rebelez, for working so hard to make me look good; you made my quilts beautiful with your expert quilting and you did it on a tight schedule

* Chris Portland, for your wise counsel and encouragement

* Cheryl Loewen and Barb Payne, for your prayers and wise advice

And finally, the most important person in my life, my husband, Rocky. Thank you, Rocky, for loving me, supporting me, and helping me do what I enjoy. I love you.

Contents

Introduction

I was hooked for life in the first grade. All it took was one brand-new box of crayons. From that first day of school until now, coloring has been a favorite activity of mine. Crayons, colored pencils, or markers—they're all fun. My two sons, when they were teenagers (enough said), would make fun of me for coloring in coloring books. I tried to explain they were coloring books for grown-ups; they just laughed. I didn't care. The coloring went on.

Add my love of fabric and quilting to my love for crayons and coloring and it seems inevitable that they would somehow eventually come together. My favorite aspect of quilting is fusible appliqué. As I fused fabric into flowers, fruit, birds, fish, and you-name-it, I found myself wanting to add more dimension, contrast, and interest to my projects. I tried several methods but they just didn't work for me. I couldn't achieve the results I wanted. One thing led to another and I decided to try crayons on my fabric. Through trial and error, practice, and suggestions from my students, I developed the Melt-n-Blend technique that I now use—and that you'll learn to do with the help of this book.

In the classroom, I've found that most people start to feel intimidated when they think they might have to paint or do anything that "real" artists do. I had the opportunity of demonstrating this technique at Quilt Expo a few years ago and a whole crowd full of fearful people stood in front of my table. I kept hearing, "It's beautiful, but I could never do that! I'm not an artist. I'm not artistic at all." They were afraid and I was frustrated. I knew they could do this. They just needed proof. I asked for a volunteer. I was going to teach somebody to color an apple right there on the spot. That's when the fear really kicked in. One second, two seconds, three seconds went by, no volunteer; I started to get nervous. Then Eleanor stepped forward with her beautiful white hair, blue dress, and sensible shoes. My guess was that she'd been coloring for about 80 years. "I've been coloring for a long time," she said. "I'd like to try this." In about three minutes Eleanor learned to color an apple. The look on her face when she colored that apple is the reason I teach and the reason I wrote this book. It's the look that says, "I did it!"

Eleanor let me keep her beautiful apple. She did it—you can, too!

Melt-n-Blend Basics

In a nutshell, the Melt-n-Blend technique is blending hot melted crayons into hot fabric. I'll teach you how to color on fabric using six coloring exercises. Each one has step-by-step instructions with photos that you can refer to as you color. It's important for you to complete all six of the exercises before beginning a project. None of the methods are hard to learn, but they do take some practice. I have taught this technique to 8-year-olds and 80-year-olds, men and women, quilters, artists of all sorts, my daughter, my mother, my sisters, and several nieces. I haven't had a single student who couldn't learn the Melt-n-Blend technique. All my students have their own touch and technique, so each project looks different, but they are all beautiful. Yours will be, too. Let the fun begin!

Supplies

When the project instructions call for "general coloring supplies," the items listed under "Coloring Supplies" are what I'm referring to. You may already have many of the following supplies on hand, but gather them all before you start coloring.

Purchasing the recommended brands will help you get the best results when coloring your projects.

Coloring Supplies

Appliqué nonstick pressing sheet, 13" x 17". The appliqués are fused to a nonstick pressing sheet when you color them. I like the Bear Thread Designs brand because it has some body and weight to it, which keeps it from moving around as you color.

Colored pencils. I use colored pencils to shade, outline, and add detail. My favorite brand is Lyra Rembrandt Polycolor. Prismacolor artists' pencils are also good. You can use any artist-quality oil- or wax-based colored pencils. These can be found at craft stores, art-supply stores, and online.

Crayola crayons. I have tried various kinds of crayons, searching for the best. Crayola crayons work better than any others, including the ones made especially for fabric. The box of 96 offers a wide selection of colors and contains all the colors you will need for any of the projects in this book. I have favorite colors and use them up quickly. I called the Crayola company and was happy to find out I could buy colors in bulk. You can order a box of 64 crayons in one color or up to four different colors for under $15. I also use Crayola Metallic FX crayons and Glitter crayons. They come in boxes of 16. You can order crayons at www.CrayolaStore.com or call 1-800-CRAYOLA.

Fabric glue. Sometimes the appliqués will not fuse securely in place, especially tiny parts like the tips of flower petals, without a bit of glue. I also use fabric glue when I miter borders and finish the binding. My choice for fabric glue is Alene's OK to Wash-It, because it's easy to find, affordable, and dependable. You can find it in almost any store that carries crafting supplies and in most quilt shops.

Fusible web. I use Steam-a-Seam Sticky Back fusible web. When fused to the appliqué fabric and the paper backing is removed, the webbing is still sticky. This is helpful when arranging several appliqué pieces together to make one unit (for instance, flower petals into a flower). Also, the appliqués will stick to the background fabric and not slip around as you arrange them. I prefer this brand of fusible web because I find it consistently dependable and easy to use, but you may want to use your favorite brand.

Fusible hemming tape. I usually use this instead of hand stitching the binding in place.

Iron. The fabric and crayon must be very hot as you color. A regular household iron or a travel iron will work, but small craft irons don't get hot enough. Those tiny little irons made for pressing in tight little places don't work well because they have such a tiny ironing surface. You need an iron that will cover a larger area. You don't need to use steam.

Iron cleaner. As hard as I try not to, I still manage to get fusible web and crayon on my iron. If this isn't cleaned off right away, it will leave unwanted crayon and black streaks on your appliqué pieces. I use Bo-Nash Iron Clean sheets. I like this brand because the sheets aren't messy, they're handy to pack around, and they're easy to use. I purchase them at my local quilt shop.

Lint roller. This handy household item is great for removing paper and crayon flecks from the appliqués.

Pencil sharpener. You'll need to sharpen both pencils and crayons. I purchased mine at an art-supply store. It has separate holes for sharpening both types of utensils.

Permanent markers. I use a black Ultra Fine Sharpie marker to trace patterns onto the paper backing of fusible web. For adding detail to appliqués, I like to use a size .02 black or brown Pigma pen. When using these pens on fabric that's colored with crayon, don't press hard or you'll damage the pen tip and the ink won't flow.

Scissors. You'll need a pair of very sharp small scissors to cut out appliqué pieces. Have a pair of regular 8" scissors on hand for larger cutting needs. This will save you time—and the edges of your small scissors!

Tabletop ironing surface. Either a board or a pad will work. Whatever you use, make sure it's large enough to accommodate the appliqué pressing sheet. A firm surface is better than a soft one, but in a pinch, I've used a bath towel folded in half.

Tracing paper. Use this for tracing patterns from the book when they need to be reversed. You'll find tracing paper in stores that carry art and craft supplies.

Blending Tools

Folded paper napkins. This is the main tool I use for blending hot crayons. I prefer Bounty paper napkins in white because after much trial and error, I found that other brands fall apart more easily and don't blend the crayons well. Don't substitute paper towels. They're good for soaking up the crayon, but they don't release it well back onto the fabric.

Blending pencil. A blending pencil doesn't have any color of its own. When you use it on top of colored pencil, it smoothes and blends the color without changing it. It can be purchased at art-supply stores, some craft stores, or online.

Stencil brush, ¼". This is my main tool for blending colored pencils. This brush can be found at craft and art-supply stores.

Very tiny stencil-like brush. I make this brush myself by taking a small round paintbrush, size 1, and cutting the bristles very short. This will give you a tiny stiff brush to blend very tiny areas. Many kinds of stores sell paintbrushes; I've found a good selection for affordable prices at craft stores. You don't need to buy high-quality artist's paintbrushes.

Washing Instructions

I don't prewash my fabric. If you do, don't prewash the fabric you'll be coloring. I've found you'll get better results coloring on fabric that has *not* been washed.

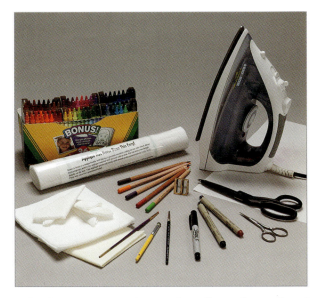

Before beginning a project, gather all supplies and tools and set up your work area as described on page 7.

However, the finished quilts can be washed. I've test-washed pieces without any disasters. Spot clean with just water if you can. If the quilt needs a complete washing, use cold water and a gentle soap made especially for quilts. Hand wash by dipping. Rinse the same way. Don't wring the water out, but instead blot between bath towels. Let the quilt dry flat; if it needs to be pressed, cover it with a clean cloth or paper napkin first.

Reversing Patterns

When tracing a pattern onto fusible web, sometimes you must reverse the image in order for it to end up facing in the correct direction after you fuse it to your quilt. For example, if a teacup handle faces to the right on the quilt, the handle needs to be facing to the left when you trace the pattern onto the paper backing of the fusible web. This is important. The appliqué patterns throughout this book have been drawn in reverse for fusible appliqué. However, for some patterns you may need to make a reversed, or mirror, image. You'll find instructions for making a reversed image in steps 1 and 2 of "Preparing an Appliqué Piece for Coloring" (page 8).

Setting Up Your Work Area

1. Center the ironing board or pad on the table in front of you, with the ironing sheet on top.

2. Place the iron on the right if you're right-handed or on the left if you're left-handed. Place fabric, fusible web, and napkins on the opposite side from the iron.

3. Place the crayons, pencils, scissors, pencil sharpener, and other supplies along the upper edge of the ironing board.

4. Place a wastebasket on the floor next to you.

Choosing Crayon and Fabric Colors

The project instructions include my crayon color choices, but you can choose others if you'd like. Generally, I choose three colors for each different object I'm coloring, plus an accent color. You'll notice in "Coloring Exercise 1" (page 13) that I use three basic colors: Dandelion, Yellow-Green, and

Tropical Rainforest Green, plus two accent colors: Wild Strawberry and Royal Purple. Using more than one or two colors will add more interest to your pieces.

You can use any color of fabric for your appliqués, including fabric with a print. Your fabric choice will affect the choice of crayon colors you can use. Light crayon colors won't show up well on darker fabrics. Some colors don't mix well. For example, you won't get a nice clear color if you use yellow crayon on purple fabric. Try the crayons on a scrap of your fabric before committing to them. The fabric I use most often is a light-yellow, 100% cotton batik. I like this fabric because it has a tight weave with a smooth surface. The crayon blends into the batik quickly and evenly. Light yellow is a good base for most crayon colors. You can use any color of crayon on it and get a nice clean, warm color. I use a bright-white, 100% cotton fabric if I want a bright, vibrant color.

Experiment with different combinations and it won't take long for you to learn what crayon colors work best with the different fabric colors. Look for fabric with a tight weave and a smooth, polished surface, like a batik. I also use batiks when using darker fabric. You can also color on prints. I have even used crayon to add depth and contrast to Sunbonnet Sue appliqués that I cut out of reproduction fabrics.

The Melt-n-Blend technique can be used with any fusible appliqué project. Notice how it gives dimension to Sunbonnet Sue. (Sue patterns by Patti-Ann Publications.)

Preparing an Appliqué Piece for Coloring

I'll teach you how to do this using a grape leaf. Whenever the pattern instructions tell you to "prepare the appliqués," you'll be following these steps. The only exceptions are when you use the Trace-n-Color or Build-n-Color techniques, as noted in the project instructions. *Note: If you don't need to reverse the pattern, skip steps 1 and 2.*

1. Lay tracing paper over the leaf pattern (page 21) and trace it with a black Ultra Fine Sharpie permanent marker.

2. Turn the tracing paper over and retrace over the lines you just made. Now the pattern is a reversed image. Mark the reversed image with an *R* or *reverse* so you can keep track of which side is reversed.

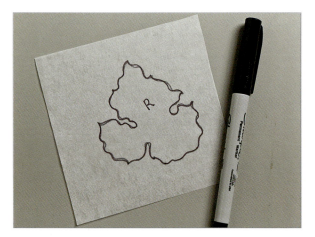

3. Cut a piece of fusible web roughly ¼" larger all around than the leaf shape. Lay the fusible web, paper side facing up, over the leaf pattern and trace it onto the fusible web with a Sharpie permanent marker. If you're preparing a reversed leaf image, place the fusible web over the pattern marked with an *R*.

4. Lay the traced fusible web on the fabric, paper side facing up, and fuse it to the fabric with your iron. If you're using a fabric with an obvious right side and wrong side, press the fusible web to the *wrong* side of the fabric.

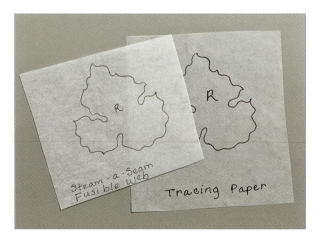

✳ Gray Shading

Use the gray shaded areas on the patterns as a guide for adding shading to your appliqués with a colored pencil. See page 15 for more details on shading.

5. Cut out the leaf using small scissors, remove the paper backing, and place the leaf on the pressing sheet, sticky side facing down. Press the leaf to the pressing sheet using a hot iron. The leaf is now ready to color.

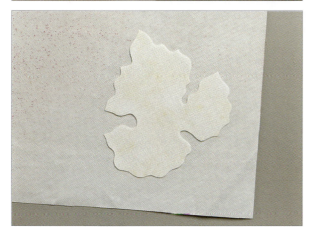

Folding a Napkin into a Blending Tool

When the instructions call for using a napkin, I'm referring to a paper napkin. The black lines shown in the photos represent the folding lines. You do not need to draw the black lines.

1. Fold the square napkin (as it comes out of the package) in half to make a triangle.

2. Fold the triangle in half to make a smaller triangle.

3. Fold two sides of this triangle toward the center, forming a pointed tip.

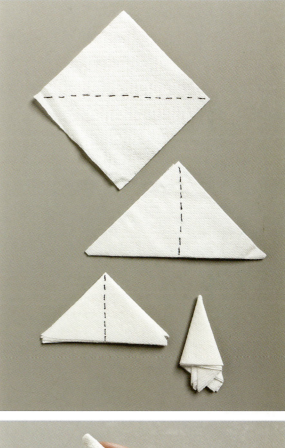

Problem Solving

From time to time, part of the process may not work out exactly as you had envisioned. Below are some of the common pitfalls and ways to avoid or fix them.

Streaky Crayon Marks

When this happens, it's generally because the fabric and crayon weren't hot enough. Perhaps they weren't heated enough before you started, or maybe they were hot enough but cooled as you were coloring.

Streaky marks

✳ The Hotter the Better!

The number one reason for less-than-great results with the Melt-n-Blend technique *is not having the appliqués and pressing sheet hot enough.* Follow the instructions carefully to avoid that problem:

1. Set your iron to the hottest setting, usually "cotton" or "linen."
2. If your iron has an auto-shut-off feature, make sure the iron is still hot before you iron. It may have turned itself off.
3. Keep your iron close by, sitting on the table next to you instead of across the room on your ironing board.
4. Fold a few napkins for blending *before* heating the appliqués and melting the crayon on the pressing sheet.
5. When you heat the appliqués and pressing sheet, hold your iron in place for a full count of 5 or 6 seconds.

   Be careful! If everything is hot enough, it will hurt if you touch your bare fingers to the pressing sheet. If doing this with children, close supervision is a must.

Small Spots of Color

Sometimes little pieces of crayon and napkin are left on the appliqué, and they cause spots when you press over the appliqué shape. Check for these and remove them with a lint-removing roller *before* you press.

Unwanted spots of melted crayon

Dark Splotchy Areas

When these occur, you're most likely pushing too hard with the napkin when you start to color. Pressing too hard dumps a lot of crayon onto the fabric all at once. Add pressure gradually so the crayon will blend evenly into the fabric.

Too much crayon in one spot

Colors Aren't Blending Evenly

Blending one color into another takes practice. Here are a few hints.

* Add pressure gently as you overlap the colors.
* Work in a circular motion rather than coloring in a back-and-forth motion.
* Make sure you overlap the edges of adjacent colors far enough so that they blend well. Don't give up!

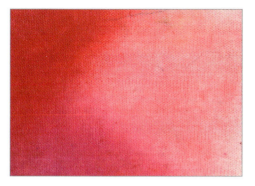

Practice blending so you won't have abrupt changes in color from dark to light, as shown here.

Muddy-Looking Areas

Using too many colors in one area or blending colors that don't mix well are two reasons for muddy results. Mixing opposites on the color wheel, such as purple and yellow or red and green, will result in a muddy color. Gray and any color or black and any color will also make brown mud. On the other hand, there may be times when you want a muddy color, for instance, for plants in a pond. To avoid getting unwanted muddy colors, blend your crayon colors on a fabric scrap before using them on your appliqués. That way you'll know for sure what color you're going to get.

If you don't like the muddy area, there are several things you can do.

* Hide the offending area by pressing a neighboring appliqué piece over it.

* Trim off the muddy part.

* Do nothing! Take a second look and reevaluate the questionable area. Just because it's a muddy color doesn't mean it's wrong. Sometimes a muddy color will add contrast to the others and make them pop out.

Where all the colors come together in the center, they mix and make a muddy gray color.

Dirty Smudges

If fusible web and/or crayon has melted onto the iron, it will come off onto the fabric when pressing. To prevent this, check your iron frequently and clean it as needed. To remove a streak from the fabric, you can try using an eraser. I use a Sanford Union gray/white eraser. The white is for erasing pencil marks and the gray is for erasing ink. I try the white side first, and if that doesn't work I try the gray side. Press lightly with the gray side; it's abrasive and can damage your appliqué. If erasing doesn't work, you may have to remake the appliqué. Don't throw away your do-overs. You may be able to use them in a future project.

Melted crayon has come off the iron onto the fabric.

Melted fusible web has come off the iron onto the fabric.

Appliqués Show through Overlapped Edges

Usually, show-through doesn't bother me. I like the added interest and depth it provides. If it bothers you, trim off the underneath parts before you fuse the appliqués to the background. Be sure to leave a tiny bit of an edge to tuck under where appliqués need to overlap.

Learning to Color

Melt-n-Blend coloring techniques are easy to learn. In this section, you'll find six coloring exercises that you can use to learn and practice the techniques before moving on to your projects. The materials list below applies to all six coloring exercises; in each individual exercise you'll find a coloring recipe to follow so you can try your hand at coloring and shading fruits and flowers in the same colors shown.

Read through the coloring instructions before you begin. In preparation, heat your iron on the cotton setting. (Remember, you don't need steam.) Take all the crayons you'll need out of the box. Because the pressing sheet gets very hot, press the appliqués close to the bottom of the pressing sheet. That way you won't have to reach across it and risk touching the pressing sheet with your hand or arm while coloring.

Refer to the patterns and illustrations for the placement of colors, shading, and details. Each coloring exercise has its own set of photos. Use the patterns (pages 21 and 22) for preparing the coloring-exercise appliqués.

Materials for Coloring Exercises

You'll need the following for the exercises in this section. The amounts listed are sufficient to complete *all* of the exercises.

* ½ yard of light-yellow batik for appliqués
* 1 fat quarter of white fabric for appliqués
* ½ yard of 12"-wide fusible web
* Scrap of medium-dark-purple batik for tulip appliqués in "Coloring Exercise 6"
* Brown colored pencil
* Black Pigma pen, size .02
* General coloring supplies (page 5)

✳ Save Time—Sort the Crayons

Take the crayons out of the box, sort them into color groups, and put them back into the box. This makes finding colors much easier and faster.

Blending

Blending colors is important for getting a good result when you color. Study the details of the close-up photo of "Orchids." You'll notice each petal has several colors, and each color overlaps the next and is carefully blended along the edges where they overlap. The colors are blended together but one color doesn't totally eradicate the other.

Notice the careful blending of colors on the petals in "Orchids."

Shading

Shading gives depth and realism to objects in your projects. The patterns indicate the areas that should be shaded. Look closely at the leaves in "Kristy's Toohoops." They look as if they're twisting and turning over because of the brown pencil I used to add shading. In reality, these twists and turns would cast a shadow depending on which direction the light is coming from. When you shade, start light and go darker slowly. Color with the edge of the pencil instead of the tip. Blend the pencil with a stencil brush.

A brown colored pencil is used to add shading, giving depth and realism to the leaves in "Kristy's Toohoops."

Coloring Exercise 1: Basic Melt-n-Blend

In this exercise, we'll be coloring a grape leaf using the basic technique.

1. Prepare the grape-leaf appliqué (page 21) using fusible web and the light-yellow batik.

2. Fold a napkin for blending the crayon.

3. Select the following crayons from the box: Dandelion, Yellow-Green, Tropical Rainforest Green, Wild Strawberry, and Royal Purple.

4. Use your iron to heat the grape-leaf appliqué to *very hot*. The pressing sheet next to the leaf will get hot also.

✳ How Hot Is Enough?

If the pressing sheet and fabric are hot enough, the crayon will quickly liquefy when it's pressed to the sheet, like butter melted to drizzle over popcorn. If your iron is heated on the cotton setting, hold the iron in place for five to six seconds to heat the pressing sheet.

5. Press the tip of the Dandelion crayon onto the hot pressing sheet, next to but not touching the leaf, and melt a puddle of crayon approximately the size of a quarter.

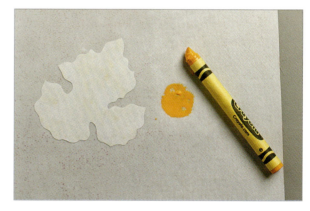

6. Press the tip of the folded napkin firmly into the melted crayon to soak it up.

✳ The Napkin Tip

When I refer to the napkin tip, use the very tip plus the next inch or so. Soak up the crayon and blend with this whole area of the napkin.

7. With your index finger, gently press the tip of the napkin onto the fabric and use a circular motion to blend the crayon over the entire area of the leaf.

8. When you're finished blending the crayon into the fabric, unfold a clean napkin and use it to cover the appliqué. Press over the napkin to remove any extra crayon and set the color.

9. Remove the napkin and use it to wipe off the leftover crayon from the pressing sheet. Now you're ready to begin with the next color. Repeat steps 2–9 when adding each new color as indicated in step 10.

✳ Reheat as Needed

The crayon and fabric must be hot as you color. If they cool before you finish coloring, follow these steps.

- Unfold a clean napkin, cover the appliqué with it, and press over the napkin.

- Remove the napkin and wipe the leftover crayon off the pressing sheet with it.

- Reheat the appliqué with the iron, melt the crayon onto the pressing sheet, and begin coloring again.

10. Melt-n-Blend the crayon colors as described below.

- Yellow-Green along the right side of the leaf

- Tropical Rainforest Green along the left side of the leaf

- Wild Strawberry and Royal Purple over small random areas of the leaf

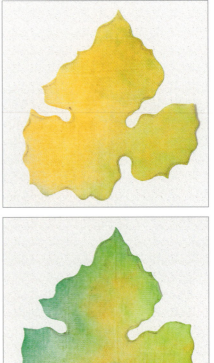

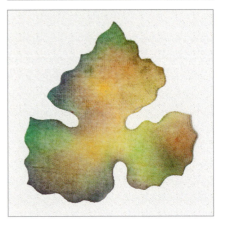

11. Outline along the edges of the leaf using a brown pencil and blend using a stencil brush.

12. Use a black Pigma pen to draw the veins on the leaf.

13. Shade over the veins using a brown pencil and blend with a stencil brush.

14. Unfold a clean napkin, cover the appliqué, and press over the napkin.

✳ Cover and Press

For every appliqué you color, the last thing you'll do is cover the appliqué with a clean napkin and press over the napkin. Always unfold the napkin first. Be sure to completely unfold the napkin so you have a single layer of paper to iron over. This allows the maximum amount of heat from the iron to get through the napkin to the appliqué. This step will not be included in the rest of the coloring instructions, but it still needs to be done.

Coloring Recipes

Now that you've learned the basic Melt-n-Blend technique, in the following exercises I'll be giving you abbreviated instructions called coloring recipes. The recipe for the leaf you just colored would look like this:

Grape-Leaf Coloring Recipe

1. Prepare the grape-leaf appliqué (page 21) using fusible web and the light-yellow batik.

2. Melt-n-Blend the crayon colors as described below:

   - Dandelion over the entire area of the leaf
   - Yellow-Green along the right side of the leaf
   - Tropical Rainforest Green along the left side of the leaf
   - Wild Strawberry and Royal Purple over small random areas of the leaf

3. Use a black Pigma pen to draw the veins on the leaf. Lightly trace over the veins using a brown pencil and blend using a stencil brush.

4. Outline around the edges of the leaf using a brown pencil and blend using a stencil brush. (After shading or outlining an appliqué with the brown pencil, always blend it with a stencil brush.)

✳ Avoid Wrist Strain

If you color for very long you may find that it puts a strain on your hands and wrists. Instead of twisting and turning your hand in different directions as you color, turn the pressing sheet; this will help keep your wrist and hand from getting tired. I cut the pressing sheet in half and color on one half. The smaller size makes the pressing sheet easier to turn as I color.

Coloring Exercise 2: More Basic Melt-n-Blend

Coloring the pear in this exercise uses the same Melt-n-Blend technique as the grape leaf in "Coloring Exercise 1," but with different details and additional shading. Although it seems repetitious, completing this exercise is important to help develop your coloring skills.

1. Prepare the pear appliqué (page 21) using fusible web and the light-yellow batik.

2. Melt-n-Blend the crayon colors as described below:

   • Dandelion over the entire pear

   • Bittersweet along the right side of the pear

   • Mahogany along the left side of the pear

   • Yellow-Green over a small area in the upper half of the pear

   • Wild Strawberry over a small area in the lower half of the pear

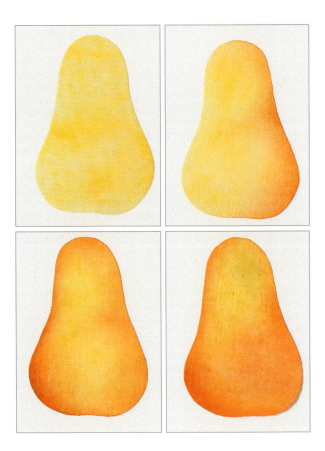

3. Outline along the edges of the pear using a brown pencil. Use a black Pigma pen to draw the details. Shade around the details using a brown pencil.

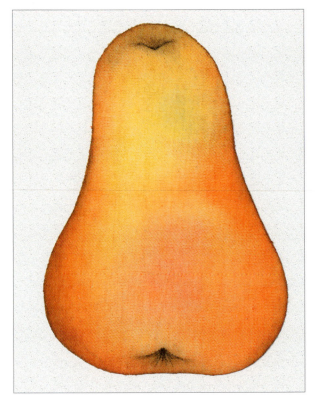

✳ *Shading Sideways*

When shading, use the side of the pencil instead of the tip. It's better to start out too light than too dark. The same goes for any of the details. Start light. You can always go darker.

Coloring Exercise 3: Color-n-Build Technique

When using the Color-n-Build technique, you prepare individual appliqué shapes, color each one separately, and then build a complete appliqué unit using those individual pieces. For example, here we'll be coloring eight separate flower petals; then we'll use those eight petals to build a whole flower unit.

1. Prepare the flower petals and center appliqués (page 21) using fusible web and the light-yellow batik.

2. Melt-n-Blend the crayon colors as described below:

   • Dandelion over the entire area of each petal

   • Yellow-Orange along the edges of each petal

   • Wild Strawberry halfway up the vertical center of each petal

   • Dandelion over the entire area of the flower center

   • Yellow Green along the edges of the center, partially overlapping the Dandelion

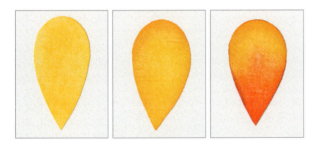

3. Outline and blend lightly along the edge of each flower petal and the flower center using a brown pencil.

4. Lay the pressing sheet over the flower pattern (page 21).

5. Peel each petal and the flower center off the pressing sheet and build the flower directly onto the pressing sheet using the pattern underneath as a guide.

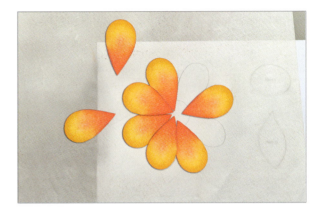

6. Unfold a clean napkin, cover the flower, and use your iron to fuse the flower pieces into one appliqué unit.

7. Peel the flower unit off the pressing sheet and set it aside to use later.

Coloring Exercise 4: Build-n-Color Technique

With the Build-n-Color technique, you prepare individual appliqué pieces, build and fuse them together into a unit on the pressing sheet, and then color the assembled appliqué unit as a whole.

1. Prepare the flower petals and center appliqués (page 22) using fusible web and the light-yellow batik.

2. Build the flower using the following steps:

   • Lay the pressing sheet over the pattern (page 22).

   • Peel the paper off the back of each petal and the flower center and build the flower directly onto the pressing sheet using the pattern underneath as a guide.

   • Unfold a clean napkin, cover the flower, and use your iron to fuse the flower shapes into one appliqué unit.

3. Melt-n-Blend the crayon colors as described below:

   • Dandelion over the entire area of the flower

   • Yellow-Green around the edges of the flower center

   • Yellow-Orange along the outer edge of each petal

   • Bittersweet halfway up the vertical center of each petal and over the tip of each petal

4. Outline around the edge of each petal and the flower center using a brown pencil. Then add dots to the middle of the flower center using a black Pigma pen. Trace over the dots using a brown pencil and lightly blend.

Coloring Exercise 5: Trace-n-Color Technique

With the Trace-n-Color technique, you trace the pattern, including the details, directly onto the right side of the fabric using a .02 black Pigma pen. After tracing is complete, you'll press fusible web to the wrong side of the fabric, behind the traced pattern, and then cut out the appliqué shape.

1. Prepare the butterfly appliqué (page 22) using the white fabric and the Trace-n-Color technique as described below.

   ✳ Cut a piece of white fabric that's at least ¼" larger all around than the butterfly pattern to be traced.

   ✳ Lay the fabric over the pattern and use a black Pigma pen to trace it directly onto the fabric, including all of the details.

   ✳ Press fusible web to the wrong side of the fabric, behind the traced pattern.

   ✳ Cut out the appliqué shape, remove the paper backing, and press the shape to the pressing sheet, sticky side facing down.

2. Melt-n-Blend the crayon colors as described below:

   • Inchworm to the inside area of the wings

   • Blue-Green to the middle area of the wings

   • Royal Purple to the outside area of the wings

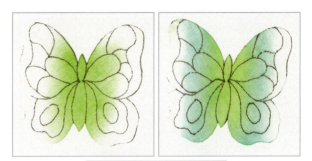

3. Color the butterfly body using a brown pencil.

4. After fusing the butterfly to the background, draw the antennae using a black Pigma pen.

Coloring Exercise 6: Variations in Fabric

With the Melt-n-Blend coloring techniques you can use any color of fabric, including fabric with a print. Keep in mind that your crayon color choices may be limited by the fabric color. An example of using different colors of fabric to color on can be seen in "Lunch? Your Place or Mine?" (below and page 76). I used medium-dark-yellow batik for most of the sunflowers, medium-dark-green batik for the leaves, and light-pink batik for the purple grapes. The vase and the fruit bowl are the original color. I added crayon around the edges for dimension and contrast.

Sunflower petals colored on medium-dark-yellow batik and leaves colored on medium-dark-green batik

Purple grapes colored on light-pink batik

In "Sunset Stroll" (below and page 74), I used an assortment of printed fabrics for the chameleon and a printed brown batik for the tree. Then I used crayon and colored pencil around the edges of the chameleon and tree to add depth and contrast. The leaves were already printed on the fabric. I cut out the leaves and used crayon to enhance and deepen their colors.

Chameleon, tree, and leaf using an assortment of printed fabrics that were enhanced with crayon, pencil, and permanent marker

For this exercise, we'll be making a tulip.

1. Prepare the tulip appliqués (page 22) using fusible web and a medium-dark-purple batik.

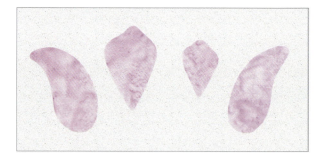

2. Melt-n-Blend the crayon colors as described below:

- Fuchsia around the edge of each petal, blending the crayon slightly into the center
- Royal Purple around the edge of each petal, partially overlapping the Fuchsia

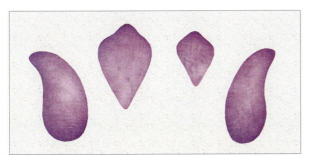

3. Build the flower, cover it with a clean napkin, and use your iron to fuse the pieces together. Then outline and blend lightly around each petal using a brown pencil.

Make 1.

Make 8.

Exercise 1
Make 1.

Exercise 2
Make 1.

Exercise 3
Flower placement guide

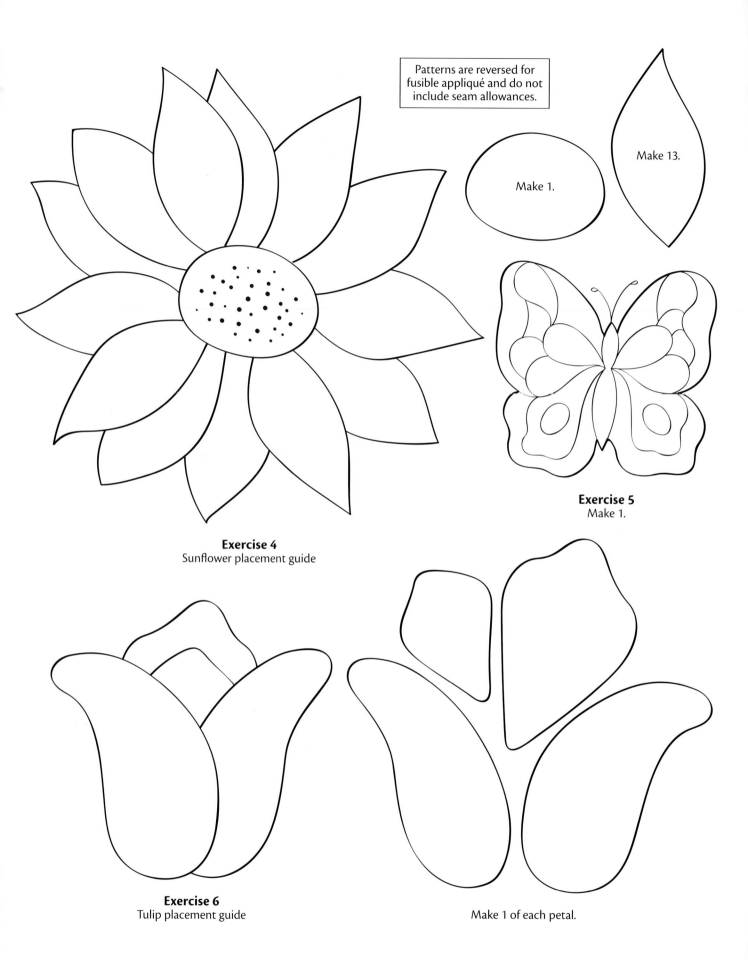

Patterns are reversed for fusible appliqué and do not include seam allowances.

Make 1.

Make 13.

Exercise 5
Make 1.

Exercise 4
Sunflower placement guide

Exercise 6
Tulip placement guide

Make 1 of each petal.

Assembling and Finishing Your Quilt

It's time to put it all together! The beautiful pieces you've so carefully colored are going to look even better when they're framed with borders and embellished with quilting. You're going to love your crayon-box quilt.

Putting the Pieces Together

Use a scant ¼" seam allowance throughout.

1. Press the background fabric. Cut the background piece the size indicated in the project cutting instructions.

2. Referring to the project photo and illustrations, arrange the appliqués on the background piece. The appliqués will shrink a little as you color and press them. Make adjustments as necessary when you arrange the pieces on the background.

✳ Tacking Saves Time

As you arrange the appliqués on the background you can use your iron to temporarily tack them in place. Place an appliqué on the background fabric; with the tip of your iron, touch the appliqué piece on a tiny spot in the center. This will lightly fuse it in place, but you'll still be able to pull it up and move it around, if needed. Since the appliqués are tacked in the center, you'll be able to slide pieces under and around each other as you arrange them. When placing pieces near the background edges, keep the ¼" seam allowance in mind. I like to work from the bottom up as I arrange the pieces on the background.

3. If the edges are showing through where pieces overlap, you can trim the underneath piece. Remember to leave a tiny edge to tuck under neighboring pieces where needed.

4. When you're satisfied with the arrangement of the appliqués, cover them with a napkin and fuse them in place with your iron.

5. Check each piece for edges that may not be fused securely and press them again. If they still won't stay fused securely in place, use a drop of fabric glue to glue them down.

✳ Removing an Appliqué

Once you've pressed a piece to the background fabric, it's pretty securely attached. However, if you feel strongly that a piece has to be removed, you can follow these steps.

1. Heat the appliqué to *very* hot.

2. Pull the piece up quickly. Be careful—don't burn your fingers. Sometimes I use a pair of tweezers. You may have to remake the appliqué, since pulling it up can distort it.

Borders

Most of the project quilts have butted corners; however, a few of them have mitered corners. You can use either method.

Borders with Butted Corners

1. Measure the quilt from top to bottom through the center. Cut two strips this length. Mark the center of the border strips and the center of the sides of the quilt top. Matching centers and ends, sew the border strips to the right and left sides of the quilt top using a scant ¼" seam allowance. Press the seam allowances toward the border strips.

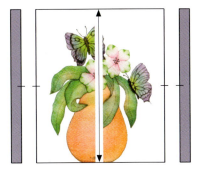

2. Measure the quilt from side to side through the center, including the borders you just added. Cut two strips this length. Mark the center of the border strips and the center of the top and bottom of the quilt top. Matching centers and ends, sew the border strips to the top and bottom of the quilt top. Press the seam allowances toward the border strips. If your quilt has multiple borders, repeat steps 1 and 2 to add each border.

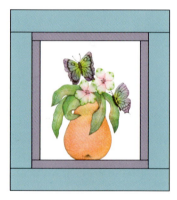

Borders with Mitered Corners

I like mitered corners because they give my quilts a matted and framed look. I used to find mitering corners harder and more time consuming than butting the corners; then I started gluing the corners together instead of sewing them. Since then I have found that mitering is actually easier, especially when adding multiple borders. Here's my method for using fabric glue to miter border corners.

1. Measure the length and width of your quilt top through the center. To each of these measurements add twice the width of your borders plus ½" for seam allowances. To be safe, add 8" to each resulting measurement to give yourself some leeway.

2. Cut two border strips to the measurement for the top and bottom borders. Cut two border strips to the measurement for the side borders.

✳ Miter as a Unit

If your quilt has more than one border, sew the individual border strips together lengthwise and treat the resulting unit as a single border strip. You'll have four border units, one for each side of the quilt.

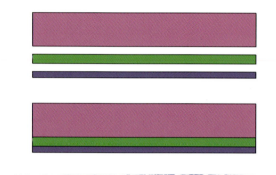

3. Find the center of each border unit and mark it with a pin. Do the same for each side of the quilt.

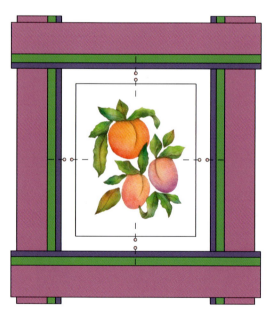

4. With right sides together, match the center of a border unit to the center of the appropriate quilt side and pin them together. Make sure to pin the edge of the *inner* border strip to the edge of the quilt.

5. After pinning the quilt centers to the border centers, gently smooth the quilt top and the borders against each other and finish pinning, making sure the raw edges are aligned. Sew the borders to the quilt using a ¼" seam allowance. Start sewing and stop sewing ¼" from the corners of the quilt center.

✳ Two at a Time

When mitering corners, I work with two border units at a time. I pin and sew adjacent border units to the quilt and miter that corner; then I pin and sew the next adjacent border, and so on. This way I don't have as much fabric bulk or as many straight pins to deal with as I sew.

6. Place the quilt on the ironing board, right side facing up. Smooth the quilt and the borders out flat. The borders will lie straight out from each other, forming a 90° angle.

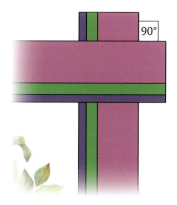

7. Fold the top border under at a 45° angle and line up the border seams. Pin them in place and press. Remove the pins and gently press the corner again. Using permanent fabric glue, apply the glue underneath the folded edge of the border. Be sure to apply the glue all the way along the edge of the fold and into the inside corner where the border and the quilt meet. Press the borders together with your fingers, making sure the border seams line up; hold the borders together for 30 seconds, and then press again with your iron. When the glue has dried completely, trim the excess fabric underneath the glued seam, leaving ¼" for seam allowances.

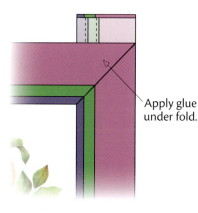

Apply glue under fold.

8. Repeat steps 4–7, sewing the remaining border units to the quilt and mitering the corners in this same way.

The Quilt Sandwich

A quilt is made up of three layers: the quilt top (or top piece of fabric), a bottom piece of fabric, and a soft layer of some sort (usually batting) in between, with all the layers being held together in some way. These three layers before they're quilted together are called the *quilt sandwich*. Once you sew or fasten the three layers together permanently, the sandwich turns into a quilt.

Selecting Batting

When I do my own quilting, I use low-loft batting in a variety of brands. To me the brand or fiber content of the batting is not as important as the loft. My quilting skills are merely adequate and thin batting makes it easier for me to get a nice result. In two of my quilts that were professionally quilted, "Garden Royalty" (page 67) and "Lunch? Your Place or Mine?" (page 76), a medium-loft wool batting was used with beautiful results. Choose the batting that's a good fit for you.

Making the Quilt Sandwich

To make the quilt sandwich, follow these steps.

1. Cut the quilt backing fabric 4" larger than the quilt top (2" on all sides). Cut a piece of batting the same size.

2. Lay the quilt back, wrong side facing up, on a table or flat surface that will accommodate its size; smooth out any wrinkles. Anchor the backing with pins or masking tape, taking care not to stretch the fabric out of shape.

3. Center the batting over the quilt back and smooth out any wrinkles.

4. Center the quilt top, right side up, over the batting and smooth out any wrinkles.

Basting

Basting holds the quilt sandwich together while you quilt it. There are several ways you can baste. You can pin the layers together with straight pins, pin the layers together with rustproof safety pins, place long stitches using a needle and thread, or use a basting spray, which is what I usually use. Keeping all layers lying flat against each other, start basting in the center and work your way out in a circular pattern, checking for wrinkles and smoothing as you go. Make sure the quilt top stays centered so that you have 2" of the batting and backing all around when you're finished basting. If you use basting spray, carefully read and follow the manufacturer's instructions for the product you use. It's important that you spray in a well-ventilated area.

Quilting

If you're going to do your own quilting, my best advice is to keep it simple. When I do my own quilting, I use monofilament thread and a simple allover stippling or meandering pattern. I don't worry about having perfect technique. I just want to do a nice, neat job that will hold my quilt together.

Binding

The binding covers the raw edges of the quilt. Choose a binding fabric that complements the quilt top and borders. I frequently bind my quilts with the same fabric used for the outer border. I like to use a folded binding and cut 2¾"-wide strips across the width of the fabric. You may have your own preferences for binding, but here's what I do.

1. Measure all four sides of the quilt and add 20" to the total. The 20" will give you enough binding to fold and miter the corners and overlap the tail ends of the binding where they eventually come together.

2. Cut the number of 2¾"-wide strips indicated for the project you're making. Sew the strips together end to end to make one long strip and press the seam allowances open.

3. Fold one end of the binding strip at a 45° angle as shown and finger-press the fold. Fold the binding strip in half lengthwise, wrong sides together, and press.

4. Starting on the bottom edge of the quilt, lay the strip on the quilt front a few inches to the left of center. Aligning the raw edges, pin the quilt and the binding strip together until you reach the first corner.

5. Beginning 5" from the end of the strip, use a ¼" seam allowance to sew the binding strip to the quilt. Stop sewing ¼" from the corner of the quilt. (If the quilt is very small, it may not be practical to start sewing the binding 5" from the end of the strip, so make adjustments as needed.)

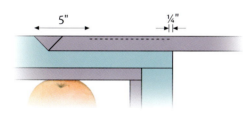

6. Remove the quilt from your machine and lay it flat. Fold the binding straight up and away from the quilt so that the fold forms a 45° angle. Finger-press the fold. Holding the fold in place, make a second fold by bringing the binding back down onto itself. Align the second fold with the edge of the quilt, finger-press, and pin both folds in place. Pin the next bit of binding strip in place until you reach the next corner.

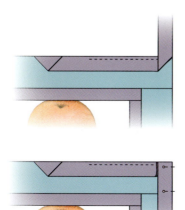

7. Begin with a backstitch at the fold of the binding and continue sewing along the edge of the quilt. Stop sewing ¼" from the corner and backstitch. Miter the corner in the same manner as before. Continue sewing the binding to the quilt and mitering each corner as you come to it.

8. Stop sewing about 6" from the point where you started and backstitch. Remove the quilt from the machine. Place the quilt on a flat surface and overlap the ending tail on top of the beginning tail. Trim the ending tail so that the overlap is 3".

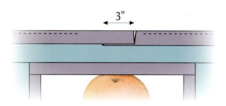

9. Tuck the ending tail into the diagonal fold of the beginning tail and glue the edges together. Hold the edges together for 30 seconds; then press with your iron and finish sewing the binding to the quilt.

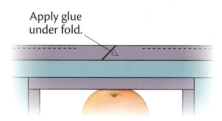

10. Fold the binding to the back of the quilt, finger-press, and pin the binding in place, making sure the folded edge covers the row of machine stitches. At each corner, fold the binding to form a mitered corner. After pinning, press the binding with your iron. Hand stitch the binding in place with a blind stitch or use ¼" hemming tape to fuse the binding in place.

Delicious

Designed and colored by Terrie Kygar. Quilted by Linda Perry. Finished quilt size: 11" x 12".

A sweet, juicy, warm pear picked right from the tree makes a delicious summer-afternoon snack. When I was about seven years old, we lived behind Great-Great-Uncle Earl. He lived in a big old Victorian house that had a big old pear tree in the backyard. His pear tree was about one minute from our front door. The pears were mine for the picking and eating any time I wanted. I ate a lot of pears that summer. This small quilt brings back good memories.

Materials

Yardage is based on 42"-wide fabric. Amounts given are generous to allow for trimming and do-overs and so you won't have to piece the borders.

1 fat quarter of light-yellow batik for appliqués and background
¼ yard of fabric for outer border
⅛ yard of white fabric for appliqués
⅛ yard of fabric for inner border
¼ yard of fabric for binding
1 fat quarter of fabric for backing
15" x 16" piece of batting
⅓ yard of 12"-wide fusible web
Dark-brown colored pencil
Black Pigma pen, size .02
General coloring supplies (page 5)

Cutting

From the background fabric, cut:
1 rectangle, 6½" x 7½"

From the inner-border fabric, cut:
1 strip, ¾" x 42"; cut into 4 pieces, ¾" x 10½"

From the outer-border fabric, cut:
2 strips, 2½" x 42"; cut into 4 strips, 2½" x 21"

From the binding fabric, cut:
2 strips, 2¾" x 42"

From the backing fabric, cut:
1 rectangle, 15" x 16"

Pear Coloring Recipe

Use the basic Melt-n-Blend technique (page 13).

1. Prepare the pear appliqué (page 31) using fusible web and the light-yellow batik.

2. Melt-n-Blend the crayon colors as described below:

   • Dandelion over the entire area of the pear

   • Bittersweet along the right side of the pear

   • Mahogany along the left side of the pear

   • Wild Strawberry over the middle, lower half of the pear

3. Outline around the edges of the pear using a brown pencil.

4. Use a black Pigma pen to draw the details on the pear.

5. Shade around the pear details using a brown pencil.

Leaf Coloring Recipe

Use the basic Melt-n-Blend technique.

1. Prepare the leaf appliqués (page 31) using fusible web and the light-yellow batik.

2. Melt-n-Blend the crayon colors as described below:

   - Dandelion over the entire area of each leaf
   - Yellow-Green along the right side of each leaf
   - Tropical Rainforest Green along the left side of each leaf
   - Wild Strawberry over several small random areas on two or three leaves

3. Shade and outline each leaf using a brown pencil.

4. Use a black Pigma pen to draw the veins on each leaf.

Pear-Blossom Coloring Recipe

Use the Color-n-Build technique (page 17).

1. Prepare the petal appliqués (page 31) using fusible web and the white fabric.

2. Melt-n-Blend the crayon colors as described below:

   - Magenta up the vertical center of each petal, starting at the pointed end of the petal, and blend toward the opposite edge
   - Yellow-Green around the edges of each petal

3. Build the flowers using five petals for each flower.

4. Using a black Pigma pen, draw in the flower-center details on each flower.

Butterfly Coloring Recipe

Use the Trace-n-Color technique (page 19).

1. Prepare the butterfly appliqués (page 31) using fusible web and the white fabric.

2. Melt-n-Blend the crayon colors as described below:

   - Inchworm to the inner area of each wing
   - Blue-Green to the middle area of each wing
   - Royal Purple to the outer area of each wing

3. Color each butterfly body using a brown pencil.

4. After the butterflies have been fused to the background, use a black Pigma pen to draw the antennae on each butterfly.

Finishing Your Quilt

See "Assembling and Finishing Your Quilt" (page 23) for detailed information, as needed.

1. Referring to the photo (page 28) for placement guidance, arrange the appliqués on the background rectangle and fuse them in place.

2. Refer to "Borders with Butted Corners" (page 23) to measure and cut the inner-border strips, and then the outer-border strips. Stitch the borders to the quilt top and press.

3. Assemble the quilt sandwich, baste the layers together, and quilt as desired.

4. Using the 2¾"-wide binding strips, make and attach the binding to your quilt.

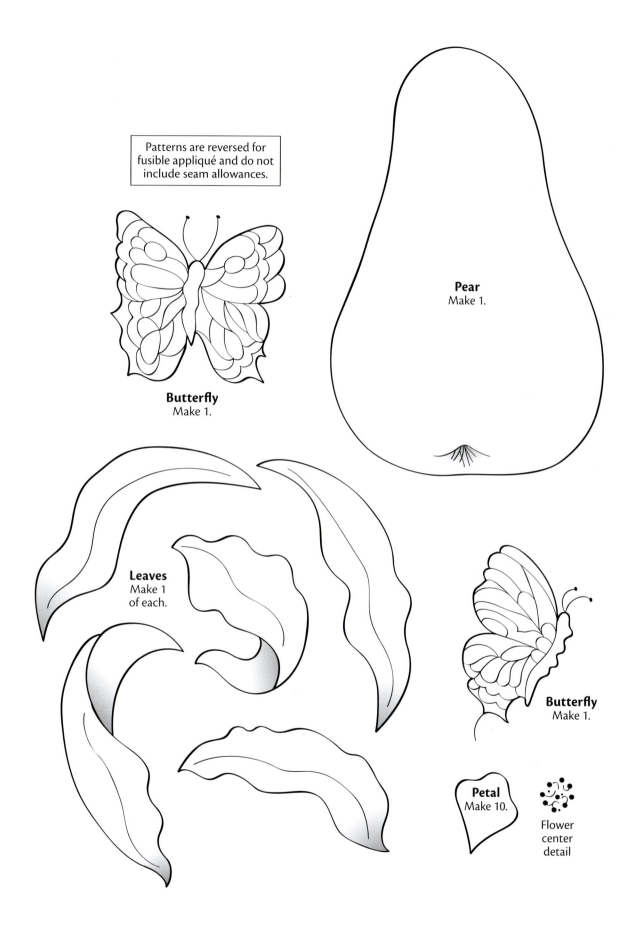

Patterns are reversed for
fusible appliqué and do not
include seam allowances.

Butterfly
Make 1.

Pear
Make 1.

Leaves
Make 1
of each.

Butterfly
Make 1.

Petal
Make 10.

Flower
center
detail

Pinwheel Flowers I

Designed and colored by Terrie Kygar. Quilted by Linda Perry. Finished quilt size: 21" x 23½".

Using a variation of the Build-n-Color technique to make a flower, one or more shapes are used over and over, overlapping each piece equally. As you overlap each piece, a secondary pattern develops. When you color over the secondary pattern, the color pops out darker. I remember as a child putting a penny under a piece of paper and coloring over it. The crayon would hit all the high spots of the penny's stamped face and transfer that likeness to the paper. This technique is similar to that.

Materials

Yardage is based on 42"-wide fabric. Amounts given are generous to allow for trimming and do-overs and so you won't have to piece the borders.

⅜ yard of white fabric for appliqués
1 fat quarter of fabric for background
⅛ yard of fabric for inner border
¼ yard of fabric for middle border
¼ yard of fabric for outer border
⅓ yard of fabric for binding
Scrap of green fabric, at least 2" x 14", for grass below flowerpot
Scrap of fabric, at least 6" x 11", for flowerpot appliqué
⅞ yard of fabric for backing
25" x 28" piece of batting
1 yard of 12"-wide fusible web
Yellow-orange colored pencil
Black Pigma pen, size .02
General coloring supplies (page 5)

Cutting

From the background fabric, cut:
1 rectangle, 13" x 14¾"

From the green fabric scrap, cut:
1 strip, 1¼" x 13"

From the inner-border fabric, cut:
2 strips, 1" x 42"; cut into 4 strips, 1" x 21"

From the middle-border fabric, cut:
2 strips, 1½" x 42"; cut into 4 strips, 1½" x 21"

From the outer-border fabric, cut:
2 strips, 3" x 42"; cut into 4 strips, 3" x 21"

From the binding fabric, cut:
3 strips, 2¾" x 42"

From the backing fabric, cut:
1 rectangle, 25" x 28"

Flower, Leaf, and Stem Coloring Recipes

Use the Build-n-Color technique (page 18) for the flowers and leaves. Use the basic Melt-n-Blend technique (page 13) for the stems.

1. Prepare the appliqués (pages 35–37) using fusible web and the white fabric. Build the leaves and the flowers, but wait to fuse the flower centers until *after* the flowers are assembled and colored.

2. Melt-n-Blend the crayon colors as described below:

Flowers A and B

- Magenta over the entire area of each petal
- Red Violet over the tip of each petal
- Red Violet over the secondary pattern

Flower C

- Cornflower over the entire area of each petal
- Navy Blue over the tip of each petal
- Navy Blue lightly over the secondary pattern

Flower D

- Violet over the entire area of each petal
- Royal Purple over the tip of each petal
- Royal Purple over the secondary pattern

Flower E

- Dandelion over the entire area of each petal
- Orange over the secondary pattern

Leaves and Stems

- Dandelion over the entire area of each leaf and stem
- Inchworm over the vertical center of each leaf and stem
- Tropical Rainforest Green along the left and right sides of each leaf and stem

Flower-Center Coloring Recipe

Use the basic Melt-n-Blend technique.

1. Prepare the five flower centers (pages 35 and 36) using fusible web and the white fabric.
2. Melt-n-Blend the crayon colors as described below:
   - Dandelion over the entire area of each flower center
   - Tropical Rainforest Green around the edges of each flower center
3. Use a black Pigma pen to draw the details on each flower center as shown in the placement guide for each flower.
4. Fuse the appropriate flower center to each flower.

Bird Coloring Recipe

Use the Trace-n-Color technique (page 19).

1. Prepare the bird appliqués (page 35) using fusible web and the white fabric.
2. Melt-n-Blend the colors for each bird as described below:
   - Inchworm to the head and throat, avoiding the beak and eye
   - Cornflower over the breast, back, upper wings, and top of head, partially overlapping the Inchworm
   - Royal Purple to the back, lower wings, and tail, partially overlapping the Cornflower
3. Use a black Pigma pen to color the eyes, leaving a small white spot in the center of each eye.
4. Color the beaks using a yellow-orange pencil.

Flowerpot Coloring Recipe

Use the Color-n-Build technique (page 17).

1. Prepare the flowerpot appliqués (pages 35 and 37) using fusible web and your chosen fabric.
2. Using a crayon color that's darker than the fabric, Melt-n-Blend the color around the edges of the flowerpot pieces.
3. Build the flowerpot as shown in the photo (page 32). Fuse the pieces together.

Finishing Your Quilt

See "Assembling and Finishing Your Quilt" (page 23) for detailed information, as needed

1. Sew the green strip to one short end of the background rectangle.
2. Referring to the photo for placement guidance, arrange the appliqués on the background, starting with the stems. Fuse the appliqués in place.
3. Refer to "Borders with Butted Corners" (page 23) to measure and cut the inner-border, middle-border, and outer-border strips. Stitch the borders to the quilt top and press.
4. Assemble the quilt sandwich, baste the layers together, and quilt as desired.
5. Using the 2¾"-wide binding strips, make and attach the binding to your quilt.

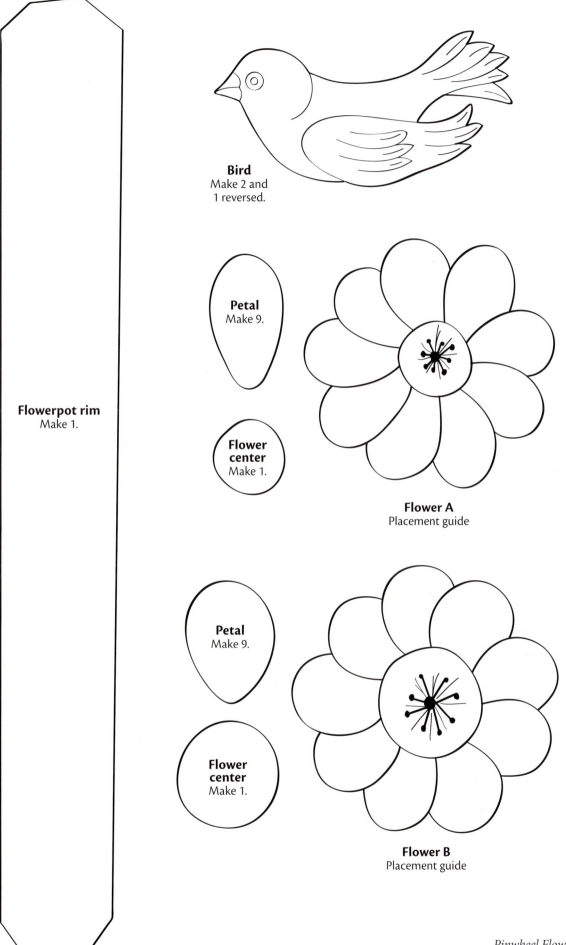

Flowerpot rim
Make 1.

Bird
Make 2 and
1 reversed.

Petal
Make 9.

**Flower
center**
Make 1.

Flower A
Placement guide

Petal
Make 9.

**Flower
center**
Make 1.

Flower B
Placement guide

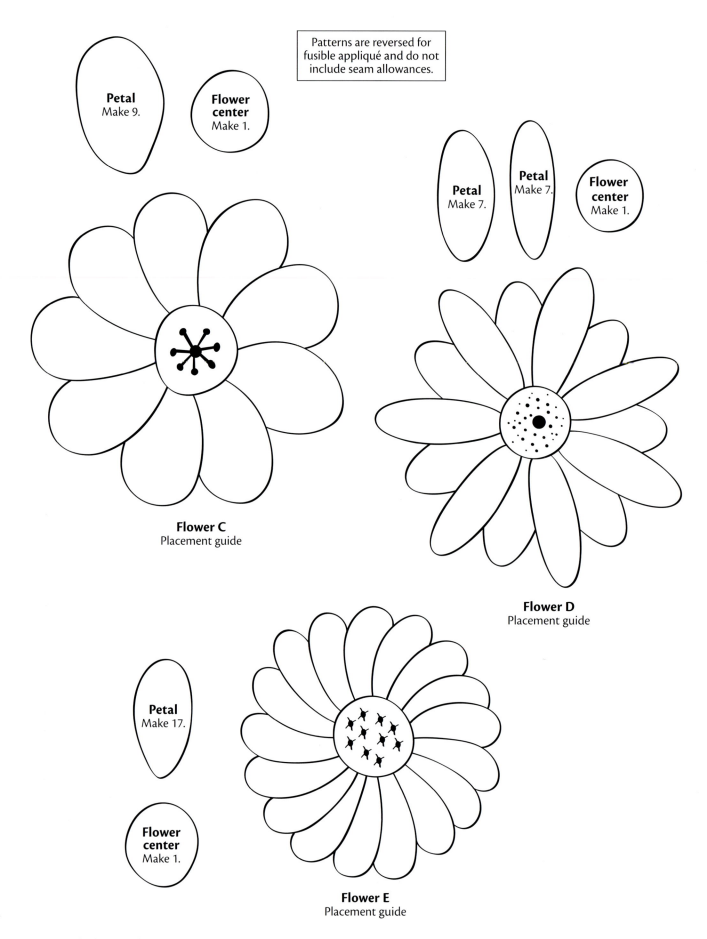

Patterns are reversed for fusible appliqué and do not include seam allowances.

Petal Make 9.

Flower center Make 1.

Petal Make 7.

Petal Make 7.

Flower center Make 1.

Flower C Placement guide

Flower D Placement guide

Petal Make 17.

Flower center Make 1.

Flower E Placement guide

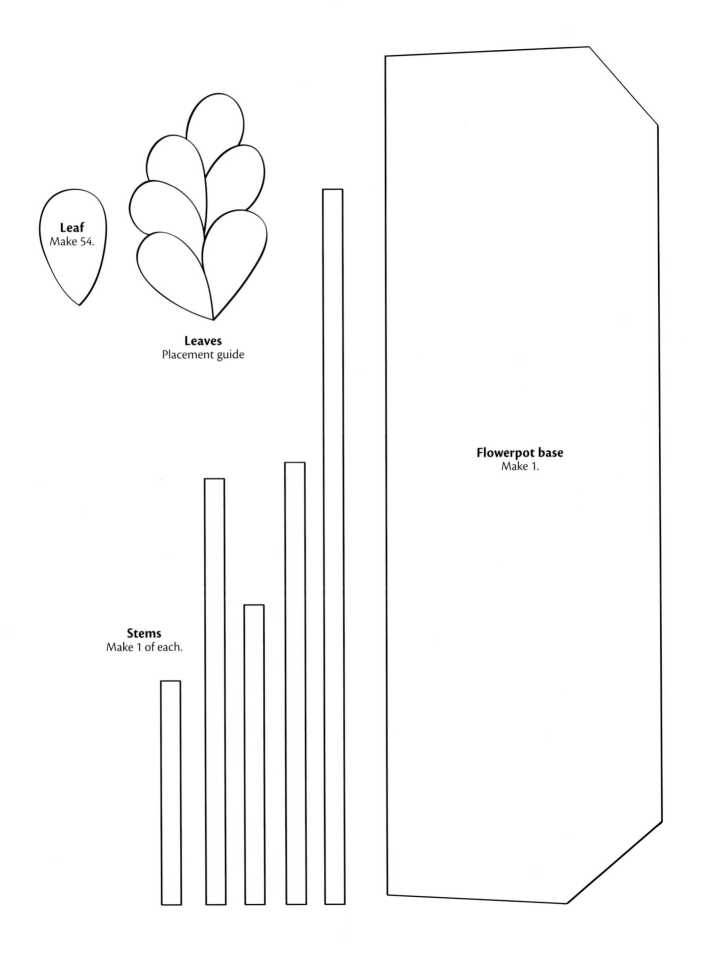

Leaf
Make 54.

Leaves
Placement guide

Stems
Make 1 of each.

Flowerpot base
Make 1.

Pinwheel Flowers II

Designed and colored by Terrie Kygar. Quilted by Linda Perry. Finished quilt size: 28" x 30".

Pinwheels are like shiny flowers that spin and whirl as they catch the wind—so simple in design, yet so delightful. These fantasy flowers remind me of the pinwheel toys I used to play with. The only thing better than a pot full of pinwheel flowers is a garden full of pinwheel flowers!

Materials

Yardage is based on 42"-wide fabric. Amounts given are generous to allow for trimming and do-overs and so you won't have to piece the borders.

1⅛ yards of white fabric for appliqués
⅞ yard of fabric for background
½ yard of fabric for outer border
¼ yard of fabric for inner border
⅛ yard of medium-green fabric for grass below flowers
⅛ yard of dark-green fabric for stems
½ yard of fabric for binding
1 yard of fabric for backing
32" x 34" piece of batting
2¾ yards of 12"-wide fusible web
Black Pigma pen, size .02
General coloring supplies (page 5)

Cutting

From the background fabric, cut:
1 rectangle, 21½" x 23"

From the medium-green fabric, cut:
1 strip, 1" x 21½"

From the inner-border fabric, cut:
4 strips, ¾" x 42"

From the outer-border fabric, cut:
4 strips, 3½" x 42"

From the binding fabric, cut:
4 strips, 2¾" x 42"

From the backing fabric, cut:
1 rectangle, 32" x 34"

Flower and Leaf Coloring Recipes

Use the Build-n-Color (page 18) and the basic Melt-n-Blend (page 13) techniques.

1. Prepare the flower petal and leaf appliqués (page 43) using fusible web and the white fabric. Build the leaves and the flowers; don't fuse the flower centers until *after* the flowers are assembled and colored.

2. Referring to the flower placement guide (page 42) and the photo (page 38), Melt-n-Blend the crayon colors and add details as described below:

Leaves

- Dandelion over the entire area of each leaf
- Tropical Rainforest Green along the outer edge of each leaf

Flowers A, B, C, and D

- Dandelion over the entire area of each flower
- Tropical Rainforest Green along the edges of each flower
- Tropical Rainforest Green lightly over the secondary patterns

- Use a black Pigma pen to draw the center detail on each flower

Flowers E and R

- Dandelion over the entire area of each flower
- Yellow-Orange over the secondary patterns
- Magenta or Wild Strawberry along the outer edges of the flowers

Flowers F, O, and P

- Fuchsia over the entire area of each flower
- Royal Purple around the outer edge of each flower

Flowers G and H

- Dandelion over the entire area of each flower
- Yellow-Orange lightly over the secondary patterns
- Magenta around the edge of each flower
- Fuchsia on a thin area on the outer edge of each petal

Flower I

- Dandelion over the entire flower
- Yellow-Orange over the secondary pattern
- Wild Strawberry over the large petals
- Red-Orange on the tip of each large petal

Flower J

- Dandelion over the entire flower
- Yellow-Orange over the secondary pattern
- Tropical Rainforest Green around the outer edge of the flower

Flower K

- Fuchsia around the inner third of the flower
- Violet around the middle third of the flower
- Royal Purple around the outer third of the flower
- Blue Violet around the outer edge of the flower

Flower L

- Yellow-Orange around the inner half of the flower
- Magenta around the outer half of the flower
- Fuchsia around the outer edge of the flower

Flowers M and Q

- Yellow-Orange around the inner third of the flower
- Wild Strawberry around the middle third of the flower
- Magenta around the outer third of the flower
- Royal Purple around the outer edge of the flower

Flower N

- Dandelion around the inner half of the flower
- Inchworm around the outer half of the flower
- Tropical Rainforest Green around the outer edge of the flower

Flower Centers G, H, K, and N Coloring Recipes

Use the Build-n-Color technique.

1. Prepare the flower-center appliqués (page 43) using fusible web and the white fabric. Build each flower center referring to the flower placement guide (page 42) and the photo (page 38) as needed.

2. Melt-n-Blend the crayon colors for each flower center as described below:

   - Dandelion over the entire center
   - Tropical Rainforest Green lightly around the outer edges of the center
   - Green over the secondary pattern

3. Use a black Pigma pen to draw the flower-center details as shown in the placement guide for each flower.

Flower Centers E, F, I, J, L, M, O, P, Q and R Coloring Recipes

Use the basic Melt-n-Blend technique.

1. Prepare the flower-center appliqués (page 43) using fusible web and the white fabric. Refer to the flower placement guide and the photo as needed.

2. Melt-n-Blend the crayon colors as described below:
   - Dandelion over the entire area of each center
   - Tropical Rainforest Green around the outer edge of each center

3. Use a black Pigma pen to draw the flower-center detail as shown in the placement guide for each flower.

Preparing the Stems

1. Prepare the dark-green fabric with fusible web.
2. Cut ¼"-wide stems in the following lengths:
   - One 16"-long stem
   - One 14"-long stem
   - One 11"-long stem
   - Two 9"-long stems
   - One 8"-long stem
   - One 7"-long stem
   - Two 6"-long stems
   - One 5"-long stem
   - Three 4"-long stems
   - One 3"-long stem

Finishing Your Quilt

See "Assembling and Finishing Your Quilt" (page 23) for detailed information, as needed.

1. Sew the medium-green strip to one short end of the background rectangle.

2. Referring to the photo and the flower placement guide, arrange the appliqués on the background rectangle starting with the stems. Fuse the appliqués in place.

3. Refer to "Borders with Butted Corners" (page 23) to measure and cut the inner-border strips, and then the outer-border strips. Stitch the borders to the quilt top and press.

4. Assemble the quilt sandwich, baste the layers together, and quilt as desired.

5. Using the 2¾"-wide binding strips, make and attach the binding to your quilt.

TOP

Leaf S   Leaf T

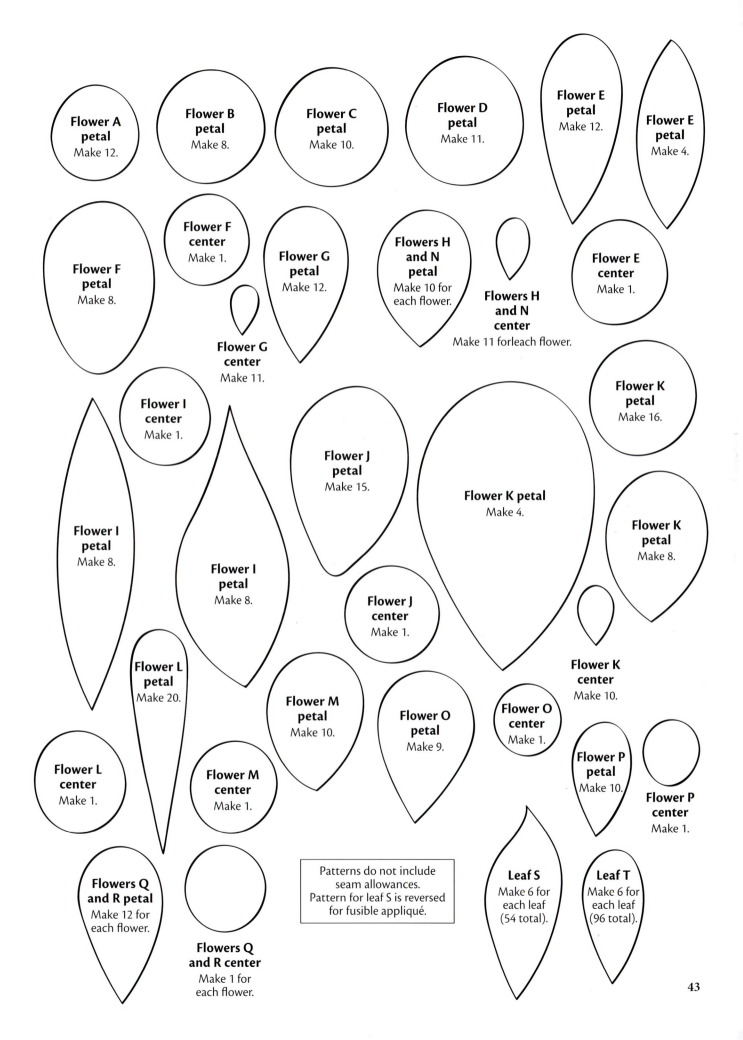

Flower A petal
Make 12.

Flower B petal
Make 8.

Flower C petal
Make 10.

Flower D petal
Make 11.

Flower E petal
Make 12.

Flower E petal
Make 4.

Flower F petal
Make 8.

Flower F center
Make 1.

Flower G petal
Make 12.

Flowers H and N petal
Make 10 for each flower.

Flowers H and N center
Make 11 for leach flower.

Flower E center
Make 1.

Flower G center
Make 11.

Flower I center
Make 1.

Flower J petal
Make 15.

Flower K petal
Make 16.

Flower K petal
Make 4.

Flower K petal
Make 8.

Flower I petal
Make 8.

Flower I petal
Make 8.

Flower J center
Make 1.

Flower L petal
Make 20.

Flower M petal
Make 10.

Flower O petal
Make 9.

Flower O center
Make 1.

Flower K center
Make 10.

Flower L center
Make 1.

Flower M center
Make 1.

Flower P petal
Make 10.

Flower P center
Make 1.

Flowers Q and R petal
Make 12 for each flower.

Flowers Q and R center
Make 1 for each flower.

Patterns do not include seam allowances.
Pattern for leaf S is reversed for fusible appliqué.

Leaf S
Make 6 for each leaf (54 total).

Leaf T
Make 6 for each leaf (96 total).

43

Designed and colored by Terrie Kygar. Quilted by Linda Perry. Finished quilt size: 25" x 32".

When our daughter was about three years old, she and her dad would take walks or go on bike rides down through the park. Like most three-year-olds, Kristy couldn't quite say some of her words just right. Whenever she and her dad came across tulips she would call them "toohoops." We, of course, thought this was the cutest thing ever. We still call tulips "toohoops" from time to time and smile at each other.

Materials

Yardage is based on 42"-wide fabric. Amounts given are generous to allow for trimming and do-overs and so you won't have to piece the borders.

⅝ yard of fabric for background
½ yard of light-yellow batik for appliqués
½ yard of fabric for outer border
⅓ yard of fabric for middle border
¼ yard of fabric for inner border
1 fat quarter of fabric for vase appliqué
Scrap of white fabric, at least 2" x 6", for butterfly appliqués
⅜ yard of fabric for binding
1 yard of fabric for backing
29" x 36" piece of batting
1½ yards of 12"-wide fusible web
Brown colored pencil
Black Pigma pen, size .02
General coloring supplies (page 5)

Cutting

From the background fabric, cut:
1 rectangle, 16½" x 23½"

From the inner-border fabric, cut:
4 strips, 1" x 42"

From the middle-border fabric, cut:
4 strips, 1¾" x 42"

From the outer-border fabric, cut:
4 strips, 3" x 42"

From the binding fabric, cut:
4 strips, 2¾" x 42"

From the backing fabric, cut:
1 rectangle, 29" x 36"

Vase and Handle Coloring Recipes

Use the Color-n-Build (page 17) and the basic Melt-n-Blend (page 13) techniques.

1. Prepare the vase appliqués (pages 47–51) using fusible web and your chosen fabric.

2. Choose a crayon color that is darker than the fabric. Melt-n-Blend that color around the edges of the vase and handle, and then fuse the pieces together.

3. Outline along the outer edge of the vase and handle with a brown pencil.

Tulips A, B, C, D, E, F, and G Coloring Recipes

You can use either the Color-n-Build or the Build-n-Color technique (page 18).

1. Prepare the petals for each tulip (pages 48–51) using fusible web and the light-yellow batik. As you trace the tulips, add a scant ¼" seam allowance to each petal edge that needs to be tucked under neighboring petals.

2. Melt-n-Blend the crayon colors as described below:

Tulip A

- Dandelion along the vertical center of each petal
- Red-Orange around the edges of each petal
- Scarlet halfway up the vertical center of each petal

Tulip B

- Yellow-Orange along the vertical center of each petal
- Wild Strawberry along the edges and slightly into the center of each petal
- Fuchsia along the edges of each petal

Tulip C

- Dandelion over the entire area of each petal
- Yellow-Orange along the edges and slightly into the center of each petal
- Orange along the edges of each petal, partially overlapping the Yellow-Orange
- Scarlet to the tip of each petal

Tulip D

- Red over the entire area of each petal
- Maroon along the edges and slightly into the center of each petal
- Chestnut to the tip of each petal

Tulip E

- Dandelion over the entire area of each petal
- Yellow-Orange along the edges and slightly into the center of each petal

- Yellow-Green along the bottom edge of the petals, where they meet the stem

Tulip F

- Magenta over the entire area of each petal
- Fuchsia around the edges and slightly into the center of each petal
- Yellow-Orange to the tips of each petal

Tulip G

- Violet-Red over the entire area of each petal
- Fuchsia around the edges and slightly into the center of each petal
- Royal Purple to the tip of each petal

3. If you used the Color-n-Build technique, build each tulip. (Skip this step if you used the Build-n-Color technique.)

4. Lightly outline along the outer edge of each tulip petal using a brown pencil.

Tulip-Leaf and Stem Coloring Recipe

Use the basic Melt-n-Blend technique.

1. Prepare the leaves and stems (pages 48–51) using fusible web and the light-yellow batik. As you trace the leaves and stems, add a scant ¼" seam allowance to the ends of the leaves and stems that need to be tucked under neighboring appliqués.

2. Use a black Pigma pen to draw the black line where the leaves bend and twist.

3. Melt-n-Blend the crayon colors as described below:

- Dandelion along the vertical center of each leaf and stem
- Yellow-Green along the right side of each leaf and stem
- Tropical Rainforest Green along the left side of each leaf and stem
- Wild Strawberry over small random areas of each leaf

4. Shade and outline each leaf using a brown pencil.

Butterfly Coloring Recipe

Use the Trace-n-Color technique (page 19).

1. Prepare the three butterflies (pages 48 and 51) using fusible web and the white fabric.

2. Melt-n-Blend the crayon colors as described below:

- Yellow-Green over the inner area of the lower wings
- Blue-Green over the outer area of the lower wings
- Magenta over the entire area of the upper wings
- Royal Purple to the tips of the upper wings

3. Color each butterfly body using a brown pencil.

4. Outline around the outer edge of each butterfly with a brown pencil.

5. After fusing the butterflies to the background, use a black Pigma pen to draw the antennae on each butterfly.

Finishing Your Quilt

See "Assembling and Finishing Your Quilt" (page 23) for detailed information, as needed.

1. Referring to the photo (page 44) for placement guidance, arrange the appliqués on the background rectangle and fuse them in place.

2. Refer to "Borders with Butted Corners" (page 23) to measure and cut the inner-border, middle-border, and then the outer-border strips. Stitch the borders to the quilt top and press.

3. Assemble the quilt sandwich, baste the layers together, and quilt as desired.

4. Using the 2¾"-wide binding strips, make and attach the binding to your quilt.

Align with patterns on pages 50 and 51.

Patterns are reversed for
fusible appliqué and do not
include seam allowances.

E

F

Align with pattern on page 49.

Align with pattern on page 50.

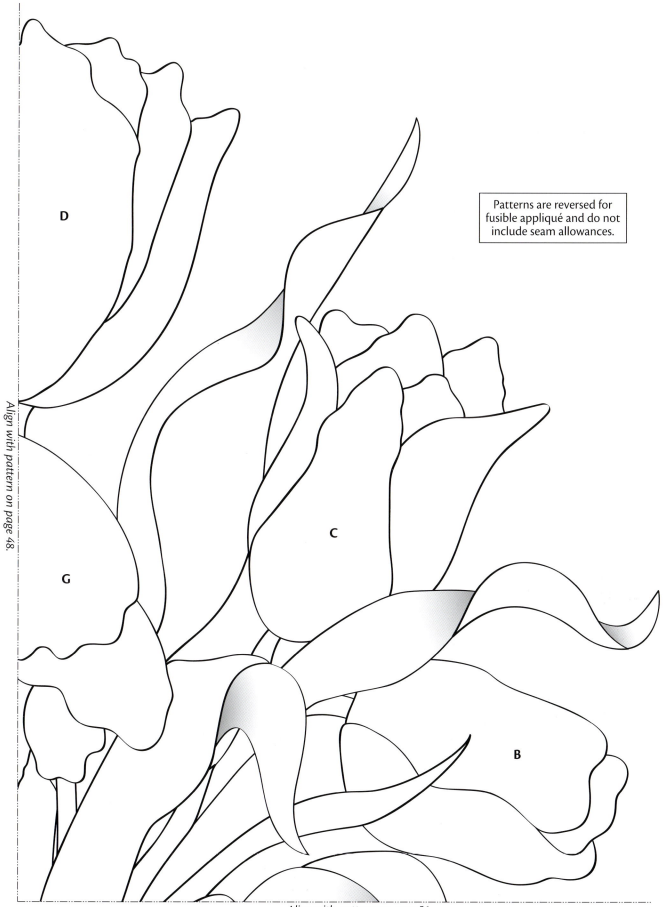

D

Align with pattern on page 48.

Patterns are reversed for fusible appliqué and do not include seam allowances.

G

C

B

Align with pattern on page 51.

Patterns are reversed for
fusible appliqué and do not
include seam allowances.

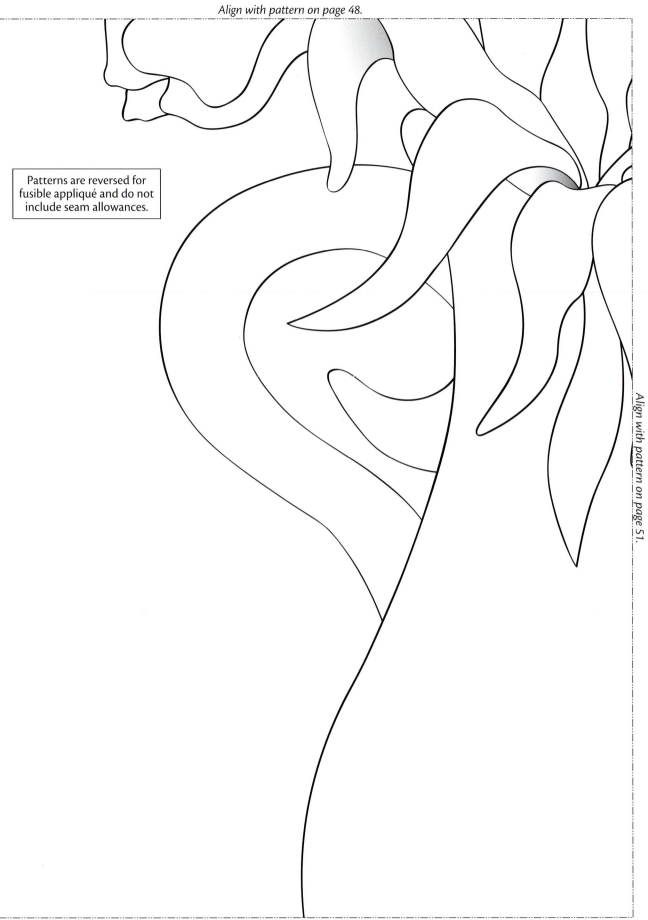

Align with pattern on page 51.

Align with pattern on page 47.

Align with pattern on page 49.

A

Align with pattern on page 50.

Patterns are reversed for
fusible appliqué and do not
include seam allowances.

Align with pattern on page 47.

Grandma's Fruit Cupboard

Designed and colored by Terrie Kygar. Quilted by Linda Perry. Finished quilt size: 16½" x 38¾".

My grandma had so many wonderful things at her house. One of my favorites was her fruit cupboard. When we had dinner at Grandma's house, she'd send me out to the back porch and I'd choose a jar of fruit for dessert. Canned fruits and vegetables in every beautiful color were there for the picking—home-canned peaches, pears, and cherries; pickled crab apples; homemade grape juice; apricots; green beans; tomatoes; pickled beets; and sweet and dill pickles. I loved Grandma's fruit cupboard.

Materials

Yardage is based on 42"-wide fabric. Amounts given are generous to allow for trimming and do-overs and so you won't have to piece the borders.

½ yard of fabric for background
½ yard of light-yellow batik for appliqués
½ yard of fabric for outer border
¼ yard of fabric for inner border
⅛ yard of fabric for sashing
Scrap of light-pink batik, at least 5" x 8", for purple grapes
½ yard of fabric for binding
1⅓ yards of fabric for backing
21" x 43" piece of batting
1 yard of 12"-wide fusible web
Brown colored pencil
Black Pigma pen, size .02
Brown Pigma pen, size .02
General coloring supplies (page 5)

Cutting

From the background fabric, cut:
3 rectangles, 8¼" x 10¼"

From the sashing fabric, cut:
3 strips, ⅞" x 42"; cut *1 of the strips* into 4 strips, ⅞" x 10¼"

From the inner-border fabric, cut:
3 strips, 1¼" x 42"

From the outer-border fabric, cut:
4 strips, 3½" x 42"

From the binding fabric, cut:
4 strips, 2¾" x 42"

From the backing fabric, cut:
1 rectangle, 21" x 43"

Peach-, Apricot-, Plum-, Apple-, and Pear–Leaf Coloring Recipe

Use the basic Melt-n-Blend technique (page 13). Use this recipe for the leaves in the apple and peach blocks.

1. Prepare the leaf appliqués (pages 57 and 58) using fusible web and the light-yellow batik.

2. Use a black Pigma pen to draw in the black line details where the leaves bend and turn over.

3. Melt-n-Blend the crayon colors as described below:

   • Dandelion over the vertical center of each leaf

   • Yellow-Green along the right and left side of each leaf

   • Tropical Rainforest Green over small random areas of each leaf

   • Wild Strawberry over small random areas of each leaf

4. Shade and outline each leaf using a brown pencil.

5. Use a black Pigma pen to draw in the veins on each leaf.

Apple
Coloring Recipe

Use the basic Melt-n-Blend technique.

1. Prepare the apple appliqués (page 58) using fusible web and the light-yellow batik.
2. Melt-n-Blend the crayon colors as described below:
   - Dandelion over the entire area of each apple
   - Yellow-Orange along the right edge of each apple
   - Brick Red along the left edge, the bottom edge, and halfway up the right edge of each apple
   - Maroon along the left edge and the bottom edge of each apple, partially overlapping the Brick Red
   - Yellow-Green over a small area in the upper half of each apple
3. Use a black Pigma pen to draw the details on each apple.
4. Shade and outline each apple using a brown pencil.

Pear Coloring Recipe

Use the basic Melt-n-Blend technique.

1. Prepare the pear appliqué (page 58) using fusible web and the light-yellow batik.
2. Melt-n-Blend the crayon colors as described below:
   - Dandelion over the entire pear
   - Bittersweet along the right side of the pear

- Mahogany along the left side of the pear
- Brick Red along the bottom and slightly up the left edge of the pear
- Yellow-Green over a small area of the upper half of the pear
- Wild Strawberry over a small area of the lower half of the pear

3. Outline along the edges of the pear using a brown pencil.
4. Use a black Pigma pen to draw in the details at the bottom of the pear, and then shade around the detail using a brown pencil.

Cranberry
Coloring Recipe

Use the basic Melt-n-Blend technique.

1. Prepare the cranberry appliqués (page 58) using fusible web and the light-yellow batik.
2. Melt-n-Blend the crayon colors as described below:
   - Dandelion over the entire area of each cranberry
   - Wild Strawberry along the right side of each cranberry
   - Magenta along the left side of each cranberry
3. Shade and outline each cranberry using a brown pencil.
4. Use a black Pigma pen to draw the details on each cranberry.

Peach
Coloring Recipe

Use the basic Melt-n-Blend technique.

1. Prepare the peach appliqué (page 57) using fusible web and the light-yellow batik.
2. Melt-n-Blend the crayon colors as described below:
   - Dandelion over the entire area of the peach
   - Yellow-Orange along the left side of the peach
   - Wild Strawberry along the right side and along the bottom edge of the peach
   - Maroon along the bottom edge and slightly up the left side of the peach
3. Outline along the edges of the peach using a brown pencil.
4. Use a brown Pigma pen to lightly draw in the center crease of the peach, and then lightly shade over the crease using a brown pencil.

Plum Coloring Recipe

Use the basic Melt-n-Blend technique.

1. Prepare the plum appliqué (page 57) using fusible web and the light-yellow batik.
2. Melt-n-Blend the crayon colors as described below:
   - Dandelion over the entire area of the plum
   - Magenta along the left side of the plum
   - Wild Strawberry along the right side of the plum

- Royal Purple along the bottom edge and slightly up the left side, partially overlapping the Magenta

3. Outline along the edges of the plum using a brown pencil.

4. Use a brown Pigma pen to lightly draw in the center crease of the plum, and then lightly shade over the crease using a brown pencil.

Apricot Coloring Recipe

Use the basic Melt-n-Blend technique.

1. Prepare the apricot appliqué (page 57) using fusible web and the light-yellow batik.

2. Melt-n-Blend the crayon colors as described below:

- Dandelion over the entire area of the apricot
- Plum along the left side of the apricot
- Wild Strawberry along the right side of the apricot
- Cerise along the bottom edge and slightly up the left side, partially overlapping the Plum

3. Outline along the edges of the apricot using a brown pencil.

4. Use a brown Pigma pen to lightly draw in the center crease of the apricot, and then lightly shade over the crease using a brown pencil.

Green-Grape Coloring Recipe

Use the basic Melt-n-Blend technique.

1. Prepare the green-grape appliqués (page 56) using fusible web and the light-yellow batik.

2. Melt-n-Blend the crayon colors as described below:

- Dandelion over the entire area of each grape
- Yellow-Green along the right side of each grape
- Forest Green along the left side of each grape

3. Shade and outline each grape using a brown pencil.

4. Use a black Pigma pen to draw the details on each grape.

Red-Grape Coloring Recipe

Use the basic Melt-n-Blend technique.

1. Prepare the red-grape appliqués (page 56) using fusible web and the light-yellow batik.

2. Melt-n-Blend the crayon colors as described below:

- Dandelion over the entire area of each grape
- Wild Strawberry along the right side of each grape
- Magenta along the left side of each grape
- Royal Purple along the left side of each grape, partially overlapping the Magenta

3. Shade and outline each grape using a brown pencil.

Purple-Grape Coloring Recipe

Use the basic Melt-n-Blend technique.

1. Prepare the purple-grape appliqués (page 56) using fusible web and the light-pink batik.

2. Melt-n-Blend the crayon colors as described below:

- Wild Strawberry over the entire area of each grape
- Magenta along the left side of each grape
- Royal Purple along the left side of each grape, partially overlapping the Magenta

3. Shade and outline each grape using a brown pencil.

Grape-Leaf Coloring Recipe

Use the basic Melt-n-Blend technique.

1. Prepare the grape-leaf appliqués (page 56) using fusible web and the light-yellow batik.

2. Melt-n-Blend the crayon colors as described below:

- Dandelion along the vertical center of each leaf
- Tropical Rainforest Green along the right side of each leaf
- Yellow-Green along the left side of each leaf
- Wild Strawberry over small random areas of several leaves

3. Use a black Pigma pen to draw the veins on each leaf. Trace lightly over the veins using a brown pencil.

4. Outline the edge of each leaf using a brown pencil.

Finishing Your Quilt

See "Assembling and Finishing Your Quilt" (page 23) for detailed information as needed.

1. Referring to the photo (page 52) as a placement guide, arrange the appliqués on each background rectangle. Fuse the appliqués in place.

2. Sew the three blocks and four 10¼"-long sashing strips together, alternating them and making sure the blocks are oriented as shown in the photo.

3. Measure, cut, and press the two remaining sashing strips. Sew them to the long sides of the quilt top.

4. Refer to "Borders with Butted Corners" (page 23) to measure and cut the inner-border strips, and then the outer-border strips. Stitch the borders to the quilt top and press.

5. Assemble the quilt sandwich, baste the layers together, and quilt as desired.

6. Using the 2¾"-wide binding strips, make and attach the binding to your quilt.

Grape leaves
Make 1 of each.

Patterns are reversed for fusible appliqué and do not include seam allowances.

Make 10 from light-yellow batik.
Make 10 from light-pink batik.

Make 8 from light-pink batik.

Make 6 from light-pink batik.

Red and purple grapes

Make 6.   Make 5.

Green grapes

Make 3.

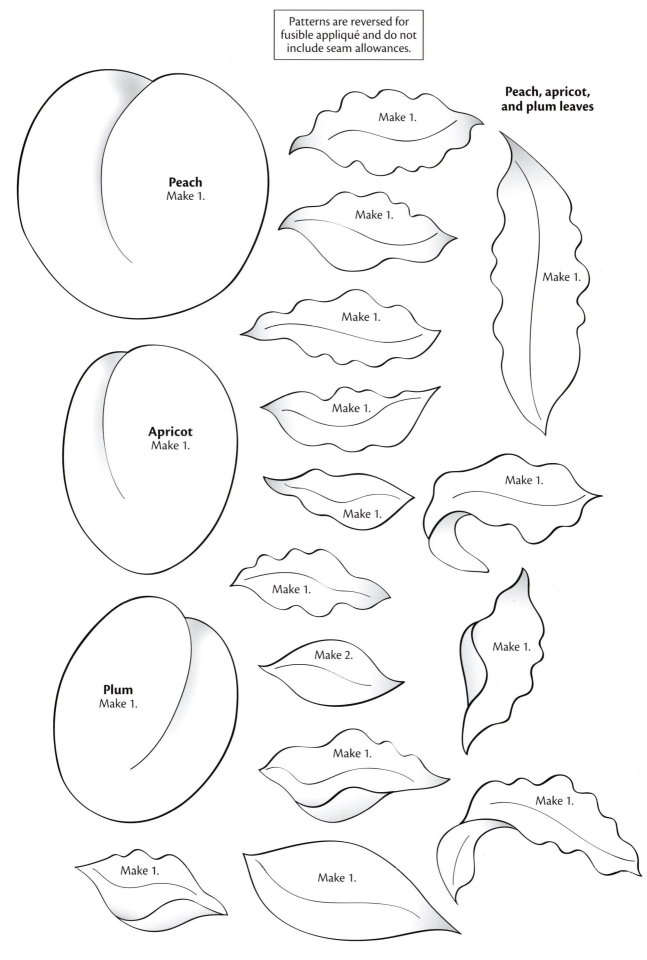

Patterns are reversed for fusible appliqué and do not include seam allowances.

Peach
Make 1.

Peach, apricot, and plum leaves

Make 1.

Make 1.

Make 1.

Make 1.

Make 1.

Make 1.

Make 1.

Apricot
Make 1.

Make 1.

Make 1.

Make 1.

Make 1.

Plum
Make 1.

Make 2.

Make 1.

Make 1.

Make 1.

Make 1.

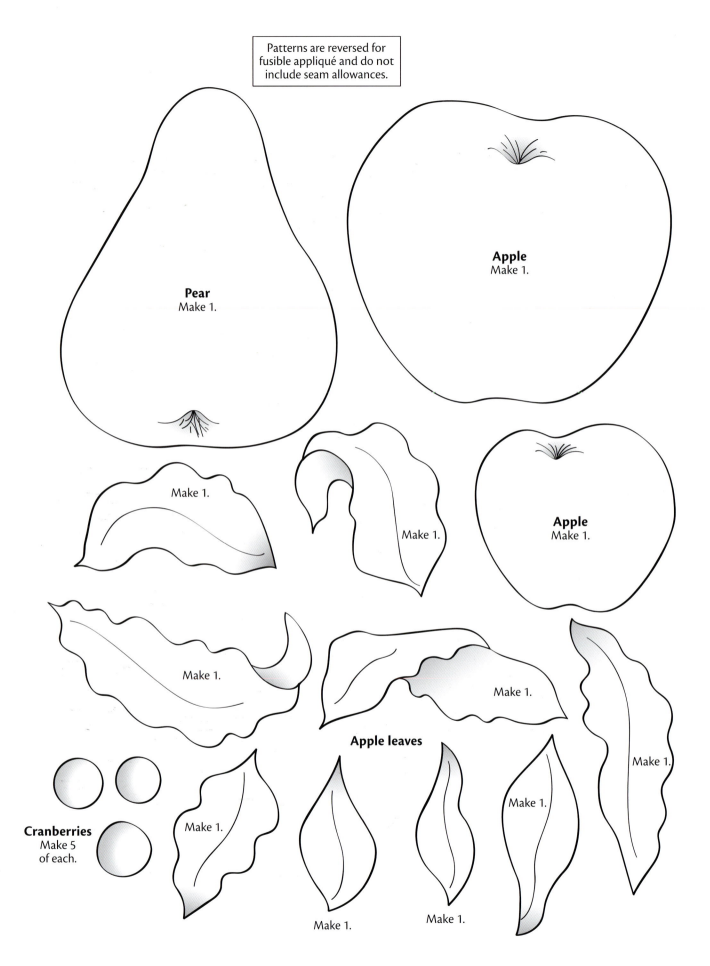

Patterns are reversed for fusible appliqué and do not include seam allowances.

Pear
Make 1.

Apple
Make 1.

Make 1.

Make 1.

Apple
Make 1.

Make 1.

Make 1.

Make 1.

Make 1.

Apple leaves

Cranberries
Make 5
of each.

Make 1.

Make 1.

Make 1.

Make 1.

Make 1.

Designed and colored by Terrie Kygar. Quilted by Linda Perry. Finished quilt size: 26½" x 29½".

Orchids are the epitome of exotic elegance. There are thousands of different kinds in every color. Their intricate parts are fascinating and make them interesting to color. It would be fun to change the colors in this quilt to purples, blues, and pinks. Try it and send me a picture. I would love to see it.

Materials

Yardage is based on 42"-wide fabric. Amounts given are generous to allow for trimming and do-overs and so you won't have to piece the borders.

1 yard of white fabric for appliqués
⅝ yard of fabric for background
⅝ yard of fabric for outer border
¼ yard of fabric for middle border
¼ yard of fabric for inner border
½ yard of fabric for binding
1 yard of fabric for backing
31" x 34" piece of batting
1¾ yards of 12"-wide fusible web
Brown, yellow-green, yellow-orange, dark-red, and dark-purple colored pencils
Black Pigma pen, size .02
General coloring supplies (page 5)

Cutting

From the background fabric, cut:
1 rectangle, 17½" x 20½"

From the inner-border fabric, cut:
4 strips, 1" x 42"

From the middle-border fabric, cut:
4 strips, 1¼" x 42"

From the outer-border fabric, cut:
4 strips, 3¾" x 42"

From the binding fabric, cut:
4 strips, 2¾" x 42"

From the backing fabric, cut:
1 rectangle, 31" x 34"

Orchids A, B, C, D, and E Coloring Recipes

Use the Trace-n-Color (page 19) and the basic Melt-n-Blend (page 13) techniques for all orchids. The numbers after each color listed correspond to numbers on the orchid patterns and refer to specific placement for each color.

1. Prepare the orchid appliqués (pages 63–66) using fusible web and the white fabric.

2. Melt-n-Blend the crayon colors and add the pencil colors as described below:

Orchids A

- Dandelion over the entire area of each orchid

- Yellow-Orange (1) over the outer half of each petal

- Violet-Red (2) partially over the Yellow-Orange

- Royal Purple (3) partially over the Violet-Red

- Yellow-Orange (4) along the vertical center of each orchid lip

- Inchworm (5) partially over the Yellow-Orange and along the lower edge of the lip on each orchid

- Color the center of each orchid using a dark-red (6) pencil
- Outline around the edges of each orchid using a brown pencil

Orchids B

- Dandelion over the entire area of each orchid
- Fuchsia (1) over the outer two-thirds of each petal
- Royal Purple (2) along the outer edge of each petal and partially overlapping the Fuchsia
- Color the center of each orchid using yellow-orange(4), dark-red (3), yellow-green (6), and dark-purple (5) pencils
- Outline around the outer edges of each orchid using a brown pencil
- Use a black Pigma pen to draw the black dots on each orchid center

Orchids C

- Yellow-Orange over the entire area of each orchid
- Red-Violet (1) over the outer half of each petal and along the outer edges of each lip
- Brick Red (2) along the outer edge of each petal and lip, partially overlapping the Red-Violet
- Royal Purple (3) on the tip of each petal, partially overlapping the Brick Red

- Color the center of each orchid using a dark-red pencil (4)
- Use a black Pigma pen to draw the line detail where the petals curl up
- Use a dark-red pencil (4) to color where the petals curl
- Outline around the outer edges of each orchid using a brown pencil

Orchids D

- Dandelion over the entire area of each orchid
- Yellow-Orange (1) over the inner half of each petal
- Forest Green (2) over the outer third of each petal
- Pine Green (3) along the outer tip, partially overlapping the Forest Green
- Burnt Orange (4) around the outer edge of the lip and about ½" toward the center
- Maroon (5) along the outer edge, partially overlapping the Burnt Orange
- Royal Purple (6) along a very thin area of the outer edge of each lip over the Maroon
- Use a dark-red pencil (7) to color the center of each orchid, adding dark-purple pencil over the red
- Outline around the outer edge of each orchid using a brown pencil

Orchids E

- Dandelion over the entire area of each orchid
- Violet-Red (1) over the outer third of each petal and the outer third of each lip
- Brick Red (2) along the outer edge of each petal and lip, partially overlapping the Violet-Red
- Royal Purple (3) along the tip of each petal and a thin area around the outer edge of each lip
- Color the orchid centers using a combination of dark-red, dark-purple, and brown (4) pencil
- Outline around the outer edge of each orchid using a brown (4) pencil

Leaf, Berry, and Stem Coloring Recipes

Use the basic Melt-n-Blend technique.

1. Prepare the leaf, berry, and stem appliqués (pages 63–66) using fusible web and the white fabric.
2. Melt-n-Blend the crayon colors and add the colored pencil as described below:

Leaves and Berries

- Dandelion along the vertical center
- Pine Green along the right side
- Forest Green along the left side
- Asparagus over random areas
- Royal Purple over random areas

Stems

- Pine Green along the right side
- Forest Green along the left side

3. Shade and outline the leaves and berries using a brown pencil. Outline along the edges of each stem with a brown pencil.

4. Lightly draw the veins on the leaves using a black Pigma pen.

Finishing Your Quilt

See "Assembling and Finishing Your Quilt" (page 23) for detailed information, as needed.

1. Refer to "Borders with Butted Corners" (page 23) to measure and cut the inner-border, middle-border, and then the outer-border strips. Stitch the borders to the quilt top and press.

2. Referring to the photo (page 59) for placement guidance, arrange the appliqués on the background rectangle, overlapping the borders along the bottom edge. Fuse the appliqués in place.

3. Assemble the quilt sandwich, baste the layers together, and quilt as desired.

4. Using the 2¾"-wide binding strips, make and attach the binding to your quilt.

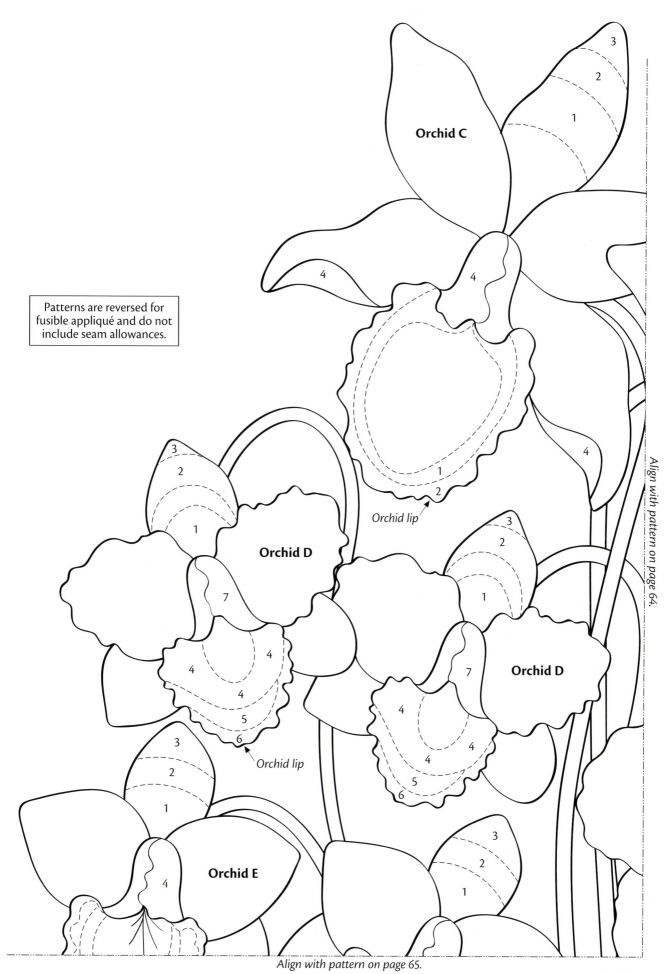

Patterns are reversed for fusible appliqué and do not include seam allowances.

Orchid C

3
2
1

4

4

4

Orchid lip

1
2

Orchid D

3
2
1

7

4
4
4
5
6

Orchid lip

3
2
1

7

4
4
4
5
6

Orchid D

3
2
1

Orchid E

4

3
2
1

Align with pattern on page 64.

Align with pattern on page 65.

Orchid C

Orchid B

Orchid B

Patterns are reversed for fusible appliqué and do not include seam allowances.

Align with pattern on page 63.

Align with pattern on page 66.

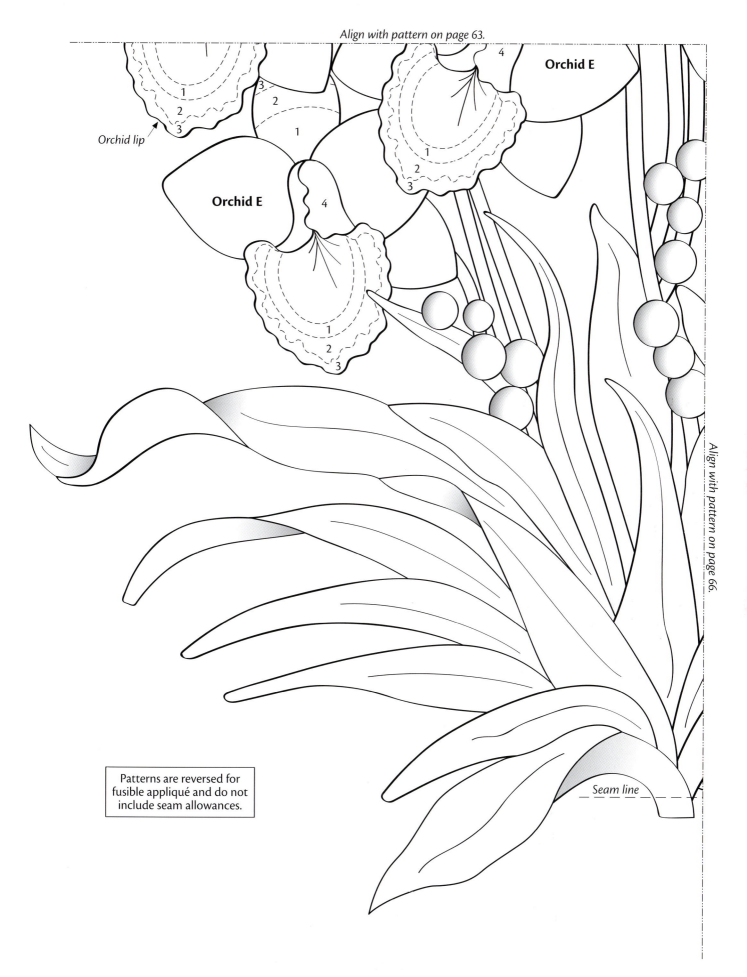

Orchid E

1
2
3

3

2

1

Orchid lip

4

Orchid E

1
2
3

4

1
2
3

Align with pattern on page 66.

Patterns are reversed for
fusible appliqué and do not
include seam allowances.

Seam line

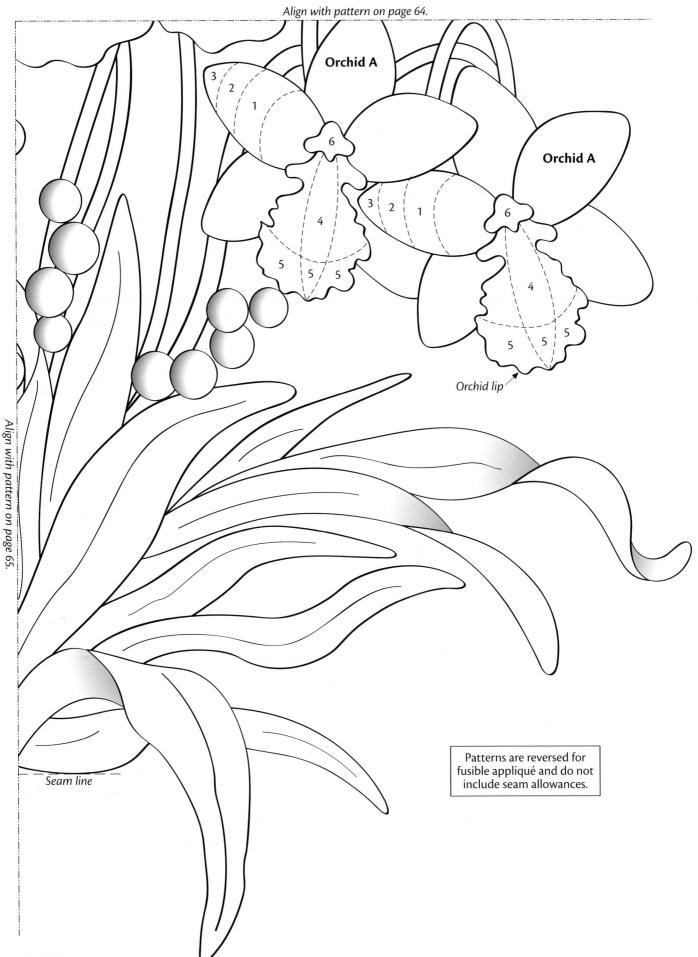

Orchid A

Orchid A

3 2 1

6

4

5 5 5

3 2 1

6

4

5 5 5

Orchid lip

Align with pattern on page 65.

Seam line

Patterns are reversed for
fusible appliqué and do not
include seam allowances.

Designed and colored by Terrie Kygar. Quilted by Kathy Rebelez. Finished size: 28" x 29¾".

We live near beautiful gardens with fields and fields of irises in every color. When we visit the gardens, the irises are gorgeous and fragrant. Set apart, standing tall and regal, their heads are way above their smaller garden subjects; they are garden royalty and everyone knows it.

Materials

Yardage is based on 42"-wide fabric. Amounts given are generous to allow for trimming and do-overs and so you won't have to piece the borders.

⅔ yard of fabric for background
½ yard of fabric for outer border
½ yard of white fabric for appliqués
¼ yard of fabric for inner border
⅛ yard of fabric for middle border
½ yard of fabric for binding
1⅛ yards of fabric for backing
32" x 37" piece of batting
1 yard of 12"-wide fusible web
Brown colored pencil
Black Pigma pen, size .02
General coloring supplies (page 5)

Cutting

From the background fabric, cut:
1 rectangle, 18½" x 21"

From the inner-border fabric, cut:
1 strip, 2" x 42"
3 strips, 1¼" x 42"

From the middle-border fabric, cut:
3 strips, 1" x 42"

From the outer-border fabric, cut:
2 strips, 4" x 42"
2 strips, 3½" x 42"

From the binding fabric, cut:
4 strips, 2¾" x 42"

From the backing fabric, cut:
1 rectangle, 32" x 34"

Iris Coloring Recipe

Use the Color-n-Build (page 17) and the basic Melt-n-Blend (page 13) techniques.

1. Prepare the iris-petal appliqués (pages 72 and 73) using fusible web and the white fabric.

2. Melt-n-Blend the crayon colors as described below:

Petals A, B, C, D, and E

- Navy Blue over the entire area of each petal
- Royal Purple along the edges of each petal
- Metallic Cyber Grape over the entire area of each petal

Petals F and G

- Yellow-Green over the inside half of each petal
- Navy Blue over the outside half of each petal
- Royal Purple along the outside edge of each petal
- Metallic Cyber Grape over the entire area of each petal

Petals H and I

- Yellow-Green along the lower third of each piece
- Navy Blue to the inner third and middle third of each piece
- Royal Purple along the upper edge of each piece
- Metallic Cyber Grape over the entire area of each piece

Petal J and Center K

- Yellow-Green over the entire area of each piece
- Tropical Rainforest Green along the edge of each piece

3. Lightly outline each piece using a brown pencil.
4. Build the iris and fuse the pieces together.

Leaf, Stem, and Stem-Top Coloring Recipes

Use the basic Melt-n-Blend technique.

1. Prepare the leaf, stem, and stem-top appliqués (page 71) using fusible web and the white fabric.
2. Melt-n-Blend the crayon colors, add the colored pencil, and draw in the details as described below:

Leaves

- Forest Green over the entire area of each leaf
- Pine Green along the right and left sides of each leaf
- Royal Purple to small random areas of each leaf

Stem and Stem Tops

- Forest Green over the entire area of the stem and both stem-top pieces
- Pine Green along the right and left sides of the stem and both stem-top pieces

3. Use a black Pigma pen to draw the black line details on stem-top A and on the leaves where they bend and turn over.
4. Trace over the stem-top details with a brown pencil. Shade and outline the leaves, stem, and both stem-top pieces with a brown pencil.

Butterfly and Hummingbird Coloring Recipes

Use the Trace-n-Color technique (page 19).

1. Prepare the butterfly and hummingbird appliqués (page 73) using fusible web and the white fabric.
2. Melt-n-Blend the crayon colors and add the colored pencil as described below:

Green Butterflies

- Forest Green over the entire area of each butterfly
- Pine Green over the entire area of each butterfly
- Navy Blue to the tips of the upper wings

Rainbow Butterfly

- Dandelion to the inner third of the upper wings
- Inchworm to the inner third of the lower wings
- Magenta to the middle third of the upper wings, partially overlapping the Dandelion
- Blue Green to the middle third of the lower wings, partially overlapping the Inchworm
- Royal Purple to the outer third of the upper and lower wings, partially overlapping the adjacent colors

Butterfly on Leaf

- Inchworm to the inner third of the wings
- Blue Green to the middle third of the wings
- Royal Purple to the outer third of the wings

Hummingbirds

- Inchworm along the top of the head, avoiding the eye, and along the back
- Blue Green along the top of the head and along the back, partially overlapping the Inchworm
- Royal Purple over the wings and tail, partially overlapping the adjacent colors
- Cerise over the breast and throat area, partially overlapping the adjacent colors
- Blue Violet to the tips of the wings

3. Color the body on each butterfly using a brown pencil. Outline each butterfly using a brown pencil. Retrace over the black lines on the butterflies and hummingbirds if they need to be darker. Color the hummingbird beaks using a brown pencil.

4. After the butterflies are fused to the background, draw the antennae on each butterfly using a black Pigma pen. Use a black Pigma pen to color the hummingbird eyes, leaving a tiny circle of white in the center of each eye.

Finishing Your Quilt

See "Assembling and Finishing Your Quilt" (page 23) for detailed information, as needed.

1. Referring to the photo (page 67) for placement guidance, arrange the appliqués on the background rectangle and fuse them in place.

2. Refer to "Borders with Butted Corners" (page 23) to measure and cut the border strips. After sewing each seam, press the seam allowances toward the just-added strips. Sew them to the quilt in the following order:

   • Sew a 2"-wide inner-border strip to the bottom of the background

   • Sew 1¼"-wide inner-border strips to the sides, and then to the top of the quilt top

   • Sew 1"-wide middle-border strips to the sides, and then to the top of the quilt top

   • Sew 4"-wide outer-border strips to the sides of the quilt top

   • Sew 3½"-wide outer-border strips to the top and bottom of the quilt top

3. Assemble the quilt sandwich, baste the layers together, and quilt as desired.

4. Using the 2¾"-wide binding strips, make and attach the binding to your quilt.

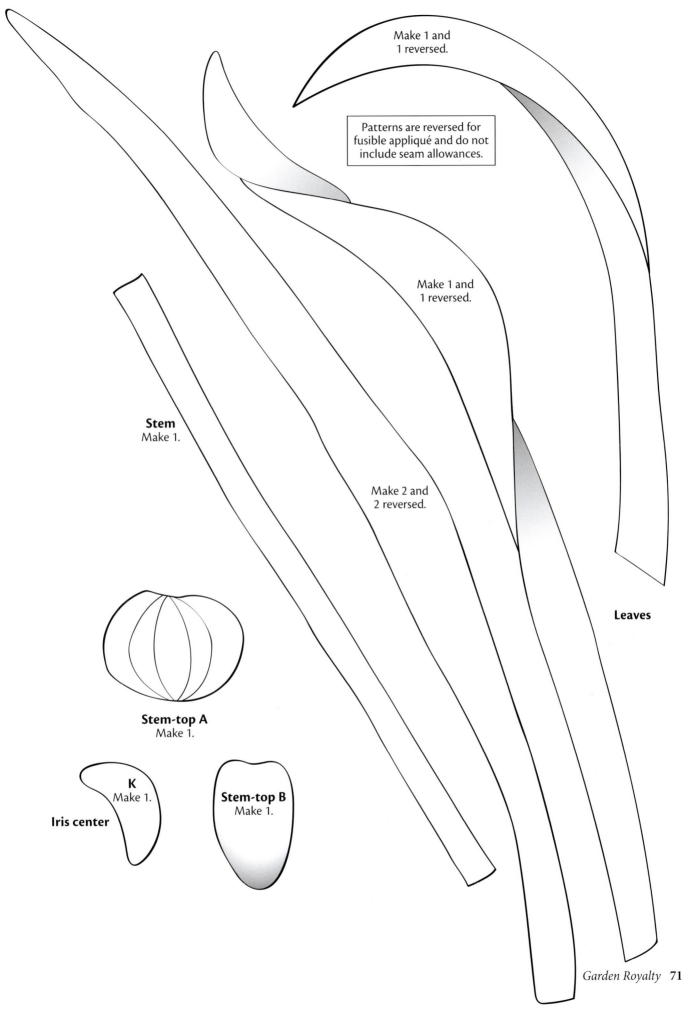

Make 1 and
1 reversed.

Patterns are reversed for
fusible appliqué and do not
include seam allowances.

Make 1 and
1 reversed.

Make 2 and
2 reversed.

Stem
Make 1.

Leaves

Stem-top A
Make 1.

K
Make 1.

Stem-top B
Make 1.

Iris center

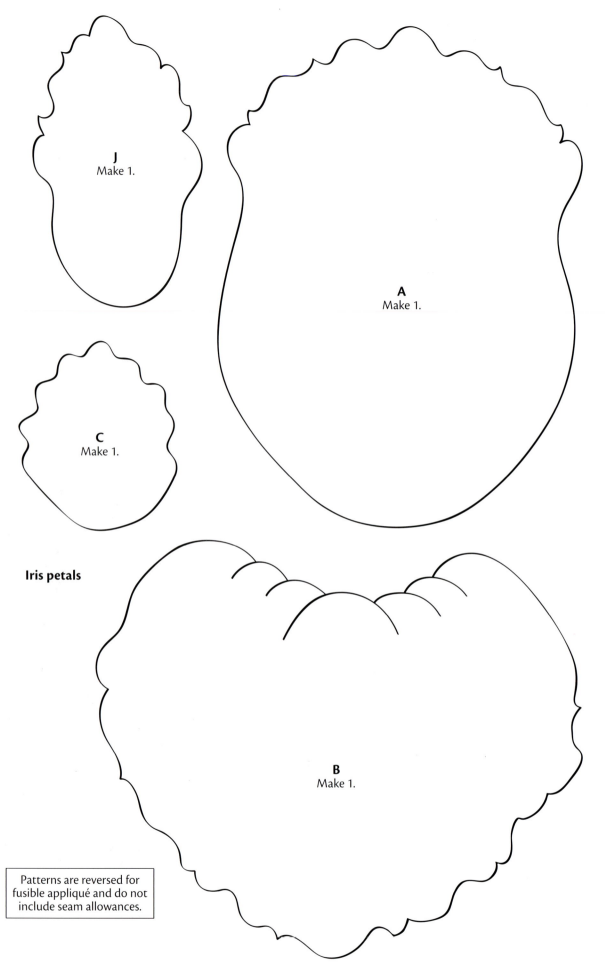

J
Make 1.

A
Make 1.

C
Make 1.

Iris petals

B
Make 1.

Patterns are reversed for fusible appliqué and do not include seam allowances.

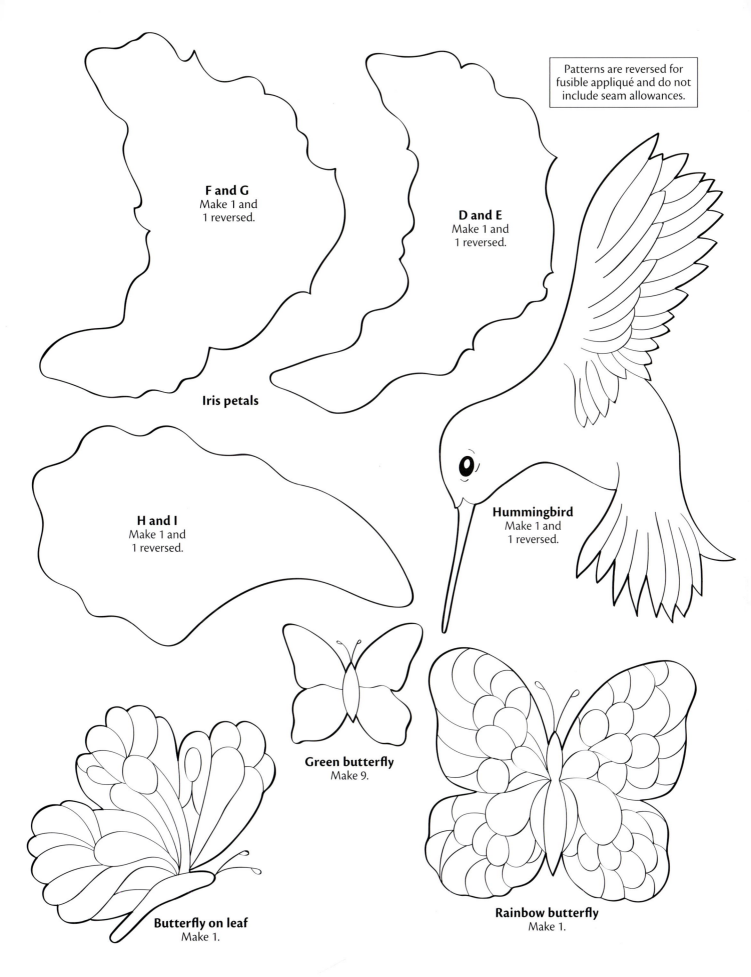

Patterns are reversed for fusible appliqué and do not include seam allowances.

F and G
Make 1 and
1 reversed.

D and E
Make 1 and
1 reversed.

Iris petals

H and I
Make 1 and
1 reversed.

Hummingbird
Make 1 and
1 reversed.

Green butterfly
Make 9.

Butterfly on leaf
Make 1.

Rainbow butterfly
Make 1.

Guardhouse
Designed, colored, and quilted by Terrie Kygar.

This quilt was one of my first attempts at using crayon to embellish my appliqués. I used a very simple, one-color Melt-n-Blend technique around the edges of the pieces. You can see that my coloring has evolved over the years. I gave this quilt to my good friend Shari. She has been evolving, too. She'd say she's getting older. I say she's getting better. Over the years she has kept guard over my family and me with her love and prayers.

Sunset Stroll
Designed, colored, and quilted by Terrie Kygar.

I wanted to give this chameleon contrast and dimension using interesting batik prints in the sunset colors he's taking on as his own. This is my first try at using crayon to embellish printed fabrics. I had a lot of fun making this guy.

Aquarium I
*Designed, colored, and quilted by
Terrie Kygar.*

This quilt belongs to my sister
and brother-in-law. They love
Hawaii and have many pictures
of snorkeling and tropical fish.
They even decorated one of
their bathrooms with tropical
fish. They keep this quilt at their
houseboat on the Willamette
River—the same houseboat
where family is always welcome.
Thanks for building so many
good memories with our family,
Shannon and Dave. I love you.

A Bird's Eye View
*Designed, colored, and quilted
by Terrie Kygar.*

This handsome guy just wants
to get a better look at the
beautiful garden he lives in.
Sometimes we can see things
better when we use someone
else's point of view.

Lunch? Your Place or Mine?
Designed and colored by Terrie Kygar; quilted by Kathy Rebelez.

Flowers and food—one or the other and many times both—are a big part of special occasions. Family, friends, food, and flowers all add up to a good time. I like to build good memories into my quilts. Sometimes as I draw, cut, and color, I think about and pray for a particular person, and then give that quilt to him or her. I'll give this quilt to my sister and brother-in-law. They host every Thanksgiving, Christmas, Mother's Day, Father's Day, Fourth of July, and Super Bowl party at their house. Thanks, Robin and Bob, for building wonderful memories for our family in the "madhouse" you call home. I love you.

Peace in the Garden
Designed and colored by Terrie Kygar; quilted by Linda Perry.

Like a beautiful garden, peace doesn't just happen. It takes time and hard work. Wisdom takes time. Humility is hard work. Peace is worth it. These were some of my thoughts when our son served in Saudi Arabia during Desert Storm.

Sharing
Designed and colored by Terrie Kygar; quilted by Linda Perry.

We all learn about sharing around the same time we open our first box of crayons. You know—all those important things for life that we were taught in kindergarten.

The Color of Love Rests in Our Hands
Designed, colored, and quilted by Terrie Kygar.

Several years ago, Grandma's Attic in Dallas, Oregon, had a quilt challenge. Rachel Greco, the owner, has this challenge every year and all the proceeds go to Sable House, a safe house for women and their children. The challenge was to complete the phrase, "The Color of Love…" Then, design and make a quilt around that phrase. Winners were selected by people's choice, and my quilt was chosen for first place. I gave this quilt to my mom. She taught me the color of love.

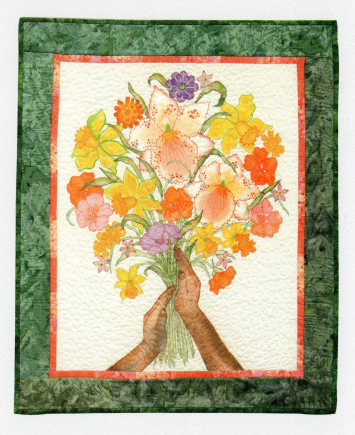

Sunny Shade
Designed and colored by Terrie Kygar; quilted by Linda Perry.

During my coloring classes, students frequently ask if I have plans for designing a pattern around this or that particular theme. Several of the most requested were pumpkins, sunflowers, and birds—cardinals in particular. I managed to squeeze all three into this sunny quilt—as well as some more fruit for me.

Hanging Out
Designed and colored by Terrie Kygar; quilted by Linda Perry.

Growing up in Oregon's Willamette Valley, I enjoyed an abundance of local fruit, including pears, apples, grapes, and berries—especially berries! As a teenager, I would pick strawberries in the summer. Lots of the kids did. Can you picture it—teenagers, picking strawberries, eating strawberries—throwing strawberries? We had fun.

Parting Words

I've given you the guidelines; now it's time for you to color outside those lines. As you develop your own technique and gain confidence, your excitement and enthusiasm will be contagious. Teach this technique to others. Help them be creative. I had a great time doing this with my family. My sisters, our mom, and several nieces were having a girls' all-night party. Sleep was optional. That evening I taught them the Melt-n-Blend technique. Women from three generations sat around the dining-room table laughing and talking while they colored pinwheel flowers. There's something about sitting around a table, working on a common project, that brings the walls down, opens up hearts, and makes communication happen. You can make that happen for people in your life around the dining-room table with a box of crayons. Hang your quilts up. Invite others over to admire them. Take pictures. Share them online. Enter your quilts in fairs, quilt shows, and challenges. Donate them to charities and fundraisers. Others will be inspired by what you've accomplished. They will gain the confidence to be creative because of what they've seen you do. Allow yourself to be the inspiration for others. It's not showing off—it's showing the way!

About the Author

I have lived most of my life in northern California and the Willamette Valley of Oregon. My grandmother first taught me to sew when I was eight years old. Mom continued to teach me, and I was making my own clothes in high school. I made my first quilt as a teenager.

I like to teach, and once had the opportunity to teach quilting and knitting to students in the fifth through eighth grades. I've often thought that if I could teach fifth-grade boys to knit and quilt, when they'd rather be doing anything but, then I could teach anybody to knit or quilt! The first quilting classes I taught were at Grandma's Attic in Dallas, Oregon, and Greenbaum's Quilted Forest in Salem, Oregon. I started out teaching watercolor quilts using fusible web, and then I taught a class on how to bend wire into cute little quilt hangers.

About that same time I started experimenting with crayons and developed the Melt-n-Blend technique for using crayons on fabric; soon I was teaching this technique to others as well. My first really ambitious crayon quilt was "A Bird's Eye View," which you can see in the quilt gallery (page 75). I made it as a class example, but Sylvia Dorney, owner of Greenbaum's Quilted Forest, encouraged me to make a pattern to go with it, which led to a few more patterns, and eventually this book.

I have a husband, two sons, one daughter, one daughter-in-law, two sons-in-law, and four grandchildren. Four of them are quilters—five if you count my husband, Rocky. He's been known to help me with quilting from time to time and has a very nice quilting stitch. My dream is to travel with my husband. I would teach and quilt and he would golf and, well, golf.

✳ There's More Online! ✳

Watch a video of Terrie's techniques and see more quilting books at www.martingale-pub.com.

Download two free patterns from Terrie at www.martingale-pub.com/extras/crayonbox.

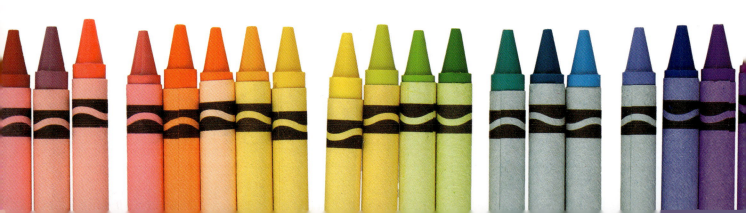